CHANGING BUREAUCRATIC BEHAVIOR

Acquisition Reform in the United States Army

CONRAD PETER SCHMIDT

Prepared for the
United States Army

Arroyo Center

RAND

For more information on the RAND Arroyo Center,
contact the Director of Operations, (310) 393-0411,
extension 6500, or visit the Arroyo Center's Web site at
http://www.rand.org/organization/ard/

In 1994, then Secretary of Defense William Perry directed the military services (Army, Navy, Air Force, and Marine Corps) to begin the process of reinventing their acquisition systems and policies. One of the most important elements of the "Perry Initiatives" was the elimination of all military specifications (milspecs) and standards from use in military acquisition. At the request of the Army, this study examines three policy questions:

- Is military specification and standard reform being implemented successfully by Army acquisition bureaucrats?

- What factors or determinants affect the willingness and ability of Army acquisition employees to implement milspec and standard reform?

- Having assessed implementation to date and understanding better what determines bureaucratic behavior, how can the Army best affect the underlying beliefs and perceptions of its personnel in order to influence behavior in support of milspec and standard reform?

To address these questions, this study applies a theoretical model of volitional behavior—called the theory of planned behavior (TPB)—to bureaucratic behavior in the Army. Based on information developed through expert interviews, a survey of Army personnel, and the application of the TPB model, the study presents a series of comprehensive recommendations on how to improve current implementation efforts.

This report is based on a dissertation accepted by the RAND Graduate School in partial fulfillment of the requirements for the degree of Doctor of Philosophy in Policy Analysis. It will be of interest to Army personnel involved with acquisition reform and its support within the Army. A related report, *Facilitating Effective Reform in Army Acquisition* (DB-233-A), by James N. Dertouzos, Conrad Peter Schmidt, Beth A. Benjamin, and David Finegold, was published in 1998. The research was sponsored by the Assistant Secretary of the Army (Acquisition, Logistics, and Technology) and the Army Materiel Command, and was conducted in the RAND Arroyo Center's Force Development and Technology Program. The Arroyo Center is a federally funded research and development center sponsored by the United States Army.

CONTENTS

Preface iii

Figures ix

Tables xi

Summary xiii

Acknowledgments xix

Chapter One
INTRODUCTION 1
Objectives of the Report 2
The Theoretical Model 3
Data Collection and Methods 3
Outline of the Report 4

Chapter Two
THE POLICY ENVIRONMENT 7
Public-Sector Reform Efforts 7
Acquisition Reform in the Department of Defense 9
Public- Versus Private-Sector Considerations 11

Chapter Three
THEORIES OF BUREAUCRATIC BEHAVIOR 13
Theoretical Approach One: Self-Interest 14
Theoretical Approach Two: Institutional Rules and
    Constraints 16
A Combined Framework for Explaining Bureaucratic
    Behavior 18

Chapter Four
    EXPLAINING BUREAUCRATIC BEHAVIOR   19
    Linking Theory to Reality   20

Chapter Five
    DATA COLLECTION   25
    Field Interview Process   25
    Field Interview Results   27
    The Army Acquisition Survey   30

Chapter Six
    UNDERSTANDING REFORM BEHAVIOR   33
    Assessing Support for Milspec and Standard Reform and
        Reform Behavior   33
    Predicting Reform Behavior   34
    Substantiating Theories of Bureaucratic Behavior   35
    Explaining Differences in Reform Intentions and
        Behavior   37

Chapter Seven
    UNDERSTANDING REFORM ATTITUDES
    WITHIN THE ACQUISITION WORK FORCE   41
    Measuring Bureaucratic Attitudes   41
    Explaining Differences in Bureaucratic Reform Attitudes .   43

Chapter Eight
    UNDERSTANDING SUBJECTIVE NORMS
    WITHIN THE ACQUISITION WORK FORCE   51
    Measuring Subjective Norms of Bureaucrats   51
    Explaining Differences in Subjective Norms Within the
        Acquisition Work Force   52

Chapter Nine
    UNDERSTANDING PERCEIVED BEHAVIORAL CONTROL
    WITHIN THE ACQUISITION WORK FORCE   57
    Measuring Perceived Behavioral Control of Bureaucrats . .   57
    Examining Differences in Perceived Behavioral Control
        Within the Acquisition Work Force   59

Chapter Ten
    ASSESSING THE ROLE OF TRAINING   63
    Reform-Related Training   64
    Participation in Reform-Related Training   67

Usefulness of Training in Changing Reform Behavior   68

Chapter Eleven
IMPROVING IMPLEMENTATION
OF MILSPEC AND STANDARD REFORM   73
The State of Implementation   74
The Importance of Behavioral Determinants   74
Recommendations for Changing Reform Behavior   76
Summary Recommendation: Use an Improved Road
    Show Training Program   87

Appendix: ANALYTIC METHODS   91

Bibliography   113

FIGURES

4.1. The Theory of Planned Behavior 20
A.1. Structural Model of Planned Behavior 93
A.2. SEM/LVM Structural and Measurement Model 93
A.3. Predicting Reform Intention and Reform Behavior
      and Standardized Coefficients in Theory of Planned
      Behavior 101

TABLES

5.1. Relevant Outcomes 28
5.2. Referent Groups Important for Determining
     Subjective Norm 29
5.3. Salient Controls 30
7.1. Differences in Belief-Based Measures of Attitude
     Across Career Group, Experience Level, and
     Organization 45
8.1. Differing Belief-Based Measures of Subjective Norms
     Across Career Group and Organization 54
10.1. Participation in Various Training Programs by Career
     Group 67
A.1. Indicator Variables Used in Measurement Model 97
A.2. Correlation Matrix 98
A.3. Covariance Matrix 99
A.4. Factor Loadings for Model Indicator Variables 100
A.5. Standardized and Unstandardized Path Coefficients
     for Structural Model of Reform Behavior, with
     Goodness of Fit Indices for Model 102
A.6. External Variables Assessed by Category 106
A.7. Prediction of Reform ATT, SN, and PBC by External
     Variables: Regression Results 109
A.8. F-Tests of Joint Significance of External Variable
     Groups 110

Recent efforts to "reinvent" government have extended to the acquisition system of the Department of Defense (DoD). In 1994, then Secretary of Defense William Perry directed the military services (Army, Navy, Air Force, and Marine Corps) to begin the process of reinventing their acquisition systems and policies. An important element of the "Perry Initiatives" was the elimination of all military specifications (milspecs) and standards from use in military acquisition. Traditional milspecs and standards were to be replaced with performance-based specifications.

The Department of the Army (Army) took the lead in implementing the new policy, directing its employees to discontinue using all milspecs and standards. By late 1994, however, Army leadership found resistance to this policy from within the acquisition work force. Although the directive appeared clear—eliminate all milspecs and standards from use—Army leadership noted that milspecs and standards were still finding their way into requests for proposals (RFPs) and statements of work (SOWs) at the core of the acquisition process. Having adopted the initiatives and seeking to implement them fully, Army leadership was interested in learning why the rank and file of the acquisition work force was not embracing the reforms. In addition, the Army was interested in identifying ways to "incentivize" or improve implementation of milspec and standard reform.

Based on information developed through expert interviews, a survey of Army personnel, and the application of a theoretical model of volitional behavior—called the theory of planned behavior (TPB)—this study identifies the key determinants of reform behavior, assesses current implementation policies, and offers a series of recommendations for improving them.

As the theory of planned behavior predicts, bureaucratic behavior in the Army turns out to be a direct function of behavioral intentions to reform and perceived behavioral control (institutional rules). It is also an indirect result of attitudes (self-interest) and subjective norms (social controls). Therefore, this study argues that Army efforts to promote reform behavior within the acquisition work force should focus first on increasing the intentions of the work force to reform. This is accomplished by changing their attitudes and subjective norms. Second, acquisition personnel will be more likely to behave in accordance with reform if they believe that the institutions and the environment facilitate the elimination of milspecs and standards.

This study further demonstrates that variations in reform behavior across the work force are a function of personal factors, such as an employee's career group, experience, organizational affiliation, and training. Specifically, when compared to military members of the acquisition work force—who are the most supportive of reform— three civilian career groups (engineering, quality assurance, and logistics) show less intent to eliminate milspecs and standards and ultimately exhibit less reform behavior. Similar results are found for employees with over 20 years' experience as compared to those with under 20 years' experience: the former have more negative attitudes toward milspec and standard reform. Conversely, employees affiliated with the program management office have higher attitude and subjective norm values when compared to those affiliated with matrix organizations. Finally, employees who attended Road Show IV, a training program focusing on procedures to eliminate milspecs and standards, and employees who have received Integrated Product Team (IPT) training have stronger (higher and more supportive) attitude values. Attending traditional acquisition management courses appears to have no effect on attitude, subjective norm, or perceived behavioral control.

While these conclusions provide valuable information on how the determinants of reform behavior vary across the work force, and thus the location of resistance within the work force, they do not tell us why the attitude, subjective norm, and perceived behavioral control values of these groups differ. To develop this information, this study examines how underlying beliefs and perceptions about milspec and standard reform vary between different elements of the work force.

First, with respect to *attitudes* of the work force toward reform, the study finds the following:

- Those with positive attitudes toward reform (military and contracting personnel) tend to believe that positive outcomes, such as a reduction in program costs or an increase in product quality, will result from milspec and standard reform. Those with negative attitudes are less willing to believe that these positive outcomes are likely. Similarly, those with positive attitudes are less willing to believe that negative outcomes (such as an increase in long-term life cycle costs) will result from reform, while those with a negative attitude see these outcomes as more likely.

- Nonmilitary personnel (engineering, quality assurance, and logistics personnel) tend to value the goals of reform (or desired outcomes such as a reduction in program costs and/or attracting commercial firms to defense work) less, contributing to their more negative attitude toward milspec reform.

- Differences in attitude between military and nonmilitary employees relate largely to differences in beliefs related to programmatic outcomes (such as product quality and cost), rather than personal outcomes (such as an increase in workload or a reduction in personal authority).

- The relatively more negative attitude of personnel with over 20 years' experience (compared to those with under 20 years' experience) is related to their belief that sustainment will be made more difficult as a result of reform.

- The relatively more negative attitude of matrix personnel (compared to program management personnel) is related to their belief that milspec reform will not result in reductions in program costs and is likely to reduce their authority in the acquisition process.

Second, with respect to the impact of *social controls* on reform behavior, the study finds the following:

- Military personnel are more likely to view various referent groups as supportive of reform, while the nonmilitary career groups (with the exception of contracting personnel) are more likely to view referents as opposed to reform. Negative attitudes are most pronounced in the quality assurance group.

- Immediate referents (such as supervisors, program managers, and co-workers) are viewed as less supportive of reform by the civilian career groups and the matrix personnel in general.

- Military personnel are more likely to view Army acquisition leaders (Assistant Secretary of the Army for Research, Development and Acquisition; and Program Executive Officers) as supportive of reform and are generally more willing to comply with these leaders than are civilian employees (engineering, quality assurance, and logistics personnel).

- Matrix personnel are more motivated to comply with matrix leadership on reform issues.

Third, with respect to *institutional rules,* the study finds the following:

- Nonmilitary employees (engineering, quality assurance, and logistics personnel) perceive environmental and organizational factors as more constraining of their ability to eliminate milspecs and standards. Military personnel view these factors as facilitating reform behavior.

- Specifically, civilians view reform policy factors (such as the training provided, information on how to eliminate milspecs and standards, the discretion provided, and information on how to work without milspecs and standards) as inadequate or constraining of the ability to eliminate milspecs.

- Civilians also view environmental factors (such as acquisition laws, availability of funds, acquisition regulations, standard operating procedures, time available, the skills of others, and the human resources available) as more constraining of reform behavior than do military personnel.

Finally, the study assesses the effects of training on the underlying beliefs and perceptions contributing to reform attitude and subjective norm. The following conclusions emerge from this analysis:

- Employees who have attended IPT and Road Show IV training are more likely to believe that milspec reform will result in positive outcomes (such as a reduction in program costs). These beliefs support a more positive attitude toward the elimination of milspecs and standards.

- IPT training appears to convince participants that important referents (such as immediate referents and Army leadership) are supportive of milspec reform. It also appears to improve their motivation to comply with these referents.

- Participation in Road Show IV does not appear to affect the underlying beliefs and perceptions that determine subjective norms or perceptions of behavioral control. Participation in IPT training does not affect the underlying beliefs and perceptions that determine perceptions of behavioral control. Traditional acquisition management courses have no effect on the underlying determinants of reform-related attitude, subjective norm, or perceived behavioral control.

Clearly, if Army leadership efforts to generate greater support for milspec and standard reform and greater employee compliance with the directive to eliminate milspecs and standards are to be successful, they must seek to change the underlying beliefs and perceptions of civilian employees. This can be done by bringing civilian beliefs into greater alignment with the beliefs of the more supportive and compliant elements of the acquisition work force—namely, military and contracting personnel. Specifically, the study recommends that the Army (1) use and improve existing training programs—IPT and Road Show IV training—to change reform attitude, subjective norm, and perceived behavioral control, and (2) target implementation efforts to the resistant elements of the work force, focusing on the alignment of underlying beliefs and perceptions between those employees who are resisting reform and those meeting implementation objectives.

ACKNOWLEDGMENTS

The completion of this report would not have been possible without the contributions of many people. While I am able to single out only a few of these contributors below, I would like to thank everyone who assisted in this effort. As always, any errors or omissions in this document are my own.

First, I would like to extend my gratitude to the men and women of the United States Army who took the time to complete my survey or sit through an interview. Without their participation, this study would not have been possible. In addition, I would like to thank the Honorable Gilbert F. Decker, Assistant Secretary of the Army (Acquisition, Logistics, and Technology), Dr. Kenneth J. Oscar, Deputy Assistant Secretary of the Army (Procurement), and Mr. Dale Adams, Principal Deputy for Acquisition, Army Materiel Command, for their sponsorship of the Arroyo Center project (to which this dissertation contributes) and for assistance in surveying 3,000 members of the acquisition work force.

Considerable appreciation must be directed to my dissertation committee. Their job was not easy, and I thank them for their time and effort. Michael Kennedy, a senior economist and my committee chairman, asked the hard questions, taught me to answer them, and guided me through the process of completing a RAND Graduate School (RGS) dissertation. James Dertouzos, a senior economist and the RAND project leader supporting this research, provided almost daily input and guidance to my research and analytic efforts. George Donohue, a deputy administrator at the Federal Aviation Administration (FAA), supported my earliest work at RAND and provided a true "policymaker's" point of view. Bryan Hallmark, a research scientist, provided invaluable insight into social psychology, its theories, and the complexities of causal modeling.

I must make a special acknowledgment of the financial support provided by the Arroyo Center and its former director, James T. Quinlivan. He—in concert with Ken Horn, director of the Arroyo Center's Force Development and Technology Program—supported not only this dissertation, but my own professional development as well. I truly appreciate their investment. In addition I owe a debt to the other members of the RAND team studying incentives in Army acquisition: Beth Benjamin, David Finegold, Mathew Sanders, and Alison Sanders. Finally, my thanks to communications analyst Donna Keyser, who played an instrumental role in converting the original dissertation manuscript into this monograph, and to Nikki Shacklett, who performed the final editing.

Chapter One

INTRODUCTION

When we use "the bureaucrat" as an epithet, we have in mind the psychological disassociation of rules about how to do one's job from the injunctions of everyday common sense ... Our system of managing in the public sector may rob the people in it of their faculties to such an extent that, like a person on a mind-numbing drug, they no longer even realize that they are missing anything.

—Steven Kelman, *Procurement and Public Management*

The reason most often given for this embarrassment of nonresults [in reforming public agencies] is resistance by the bureaucracy. Of course no one likes to be reinvented by fiat from above.

—Peter F. Drucker, in *The Atlantic Monthly*

This examination of bureaucratic behavior is intended to help policymakers better understand what motivates a bureaucrat to support and enact changes in bureau operating processes and policy. Which factors are important in determining whether or not a bureaucrat will support and implement a major change in policy? To what degree do these factors result from our system of managing in the public sector, and to what degree from other determinants? How can understanding the determinants of bureaucratic behavior assist us in implementing major changes within a bureaucratic organization?

In addressing these questions, this report focuses on the organizations and personnel involved in the acquisition of goods and services for the U.S. Department of the Army (hereafter referred to as the U.S. Army or Army). The U.S. Army is attempting major reform of its acquisition processes. Successful implementation of these changes will rely on the cooperation and discretion of thousands of federal bureaucrats who were inculcated, trained, and fostered within a hierarchical, rule-driven, and some would say excessively risk-averse organization. The challenge is to determine how important this bureaucratic environment is in determining reform behavior.

It is important to note at the outset that the terms "bureaucracy" and "bureaucrat" are used here in their purest sense, as Max Weber meant them to be applied—to denote an organizational system based on hierarchy and rules and those who work within it (Weber, 1962). Throughout the research process, the author has found the bureaucrats within the Army acquisition system to be dedicated, hardworking, and motivated individuals.

OBJECTIVES OF THE REPORT

This report addresses three policy questions:

- Are military specification (hereafter called milspec) and standard reform being implemented successfully by Army acquisition bureaucrats?

- What factors or determinants affect the willingness and ability of Army acquisition employees to implement milspec and standard reform?

- Having assessed implementation to date and understanding better what determines bureaucratic behavior, how can the Army best affect the underlying beliefs and perceptions of its personnel in order to influence behavior in support of milspec and standard reform?

Ideally, the insights gained by answering these questions will provide the Army with more and better information about what motivates its employees and affects their behavior. In this way, current implementation policies can be assessed and improvements suggested.

THE THEORETICAL MODEL

Three sets of factors are hypothesized to affect the willingness and ability of Army acquisition employees to implement reform. These factors are: (1) employees' attitudes toward implementing reform; (2) employees' subjective norms—or the perceived effect of the views of other social referents (colleagues, superiors, interest groups)—toward implementing reform; and (3) employees' perception of behavioral control—or their perception of how factors beyond their control (organizational or environmental factors) affect their ability to implement reform. These factors form the core of the theory of planned behavior (TPB), a widely tested and applied theory from social psychology (Ajzen, 1991).

These three key factors—attitude, subjective norm, and perceived behavioral control—are themselves determined by a series of beliefs and perceptions, or underlying subfactors. These subfactors are also examined in order to understand better why employees do or do not support and implement reform. For example, attitudes are derived from evaluations of potential consequences that can result from specific behaviors. If the underlying subfactors related to these consequences are favorable, a favorable attitude results and an employee is more likely to implement reform.

Application of the theory of planned behavior to the problem of reform behavior among Army acquisition employees leads to a behavioral model that identifies the factors affecting bureaucratic decisions, predicts bureaucratic behavior, and allows the development of conclusions and policy recommendations related to the implementation of reform.

DATA COLLECTION AND METHODS

To collect and analyze the data necessary to address the policy questions outlined above, a multimethod research approach was used. The first method involves a series of interviews and case studies within the Army acquisition bureaucracy. These interviews provide data and observations related to the existing reform efforts, the environment (organizational and otherwise) within which the reforms are being attempted, and the motivations and concerns of Army bureaucrats facing the new policies and procedures.

These interviews are then used to develop the second phase of data collection—a comprehensive survey administered to the Army acquisition work force. The survey is designed to provide data on bureaucratic behavior and the various factors and underlying subfactors postulated to affect behavior. These data allow for the empirical testing of the TPB model.

OUTLINE OF THE REPORT

Chapter Two describes the policy environment within which Army reform is taking place. The 1990s have seen a rise in public-sector reform efforts. These efforts, sometimes called "reinventing government," try to apply private-sector management techniques to the public sector. In many respects these reforms call for greater innovation and discretion on the part of public agencies and their employees. These same objectives are evident in the Army's acquisition reform efforts. While these reforms hold promise, there are concerns about the applicability of private-sector techniques for the public sector, as well as the formidable bureaucratic barriers that must be overcome if they are to operate effectively.

Chapter Three examines two broad theoretical approaches to why bureaucracies and bureaucrats operate the way they do across a variety of disciplinary boundaries, including public administration, political science, organizational theory, and economics. Each of the theories considers the prime motivation or objective of the bureaucrat and his/her organization as being either self-interest or institutional rules and constraints. These theories provide a framework for viewing and assessing the functioning of the Army acquisition bureaucracy.

Chapter Four outlines the theory of planned behavior and uses it to establish a notional model of bureaucratic behavior (Ajzen, 1991). This model is used to operationalize and test the determinants of bureaucratic behavior as they apply in the Army acquisition bureaucracy.

Chapter Five first describes the process of data collection, including 84 field interviews with a wide range of acquisition personnel on acquisition reform and milspec and standard reform. These data are useful for identifying the underlying subfactors that may be important in determining employees' attitudes, subjective norms, and perceptions of behavioral control. The chapter then describes an Army acquisition survey administered to 3,000 randomly selected members of the acquisition work force.

Chapter Six provides an initial analysis of the state of support for reform, and the state of reform behavior, within the acquisition work force. It also describes the application of the bureaucratic behavior model using the survey data from the Army acquisition work force. This model identifies the importance and relative strength of bureaucratic attitudes, subjective norms (beliefs about referents), and perceptions of behavioral control (how difficult it will be to reform) in the prediction of bureaucratic behavior. In addition, this chapter examines how these three factors vary as a function of a bureaucrat's experience, profession, and other individual characteristics.

Chapter Seven examines the role of underlying subfactors in the formation of bureaucratic attitudes toward milspec and standard reform. Specifically, the underlying subfactors of those who have a favorable attitude toward reform are compared with those employees with a less favorable attitude toward reform. This comparison provides information on why the attitudes of these groups differ and helps us understand why their behavior might differ as well.

Chapter Eight examines another set of underlying subfactors and their impact on the subjective norms held by Army acquisition employees—or what bureaucrats believe important referents want them to do. Specifically, this chapter examines how different members of the acquisition work force view important referent groups. Do some groups believe specific referents support reform while others view these referents as opposed? Comparing the underlying subfactors of those employees with a positive subjective norm to those with a negative subjective norm may make it possible to better understand why behaviors differ.

Chapter Nine examines the role of underlying subfactors in the formation of perceptions of behavioral control—or how difficult bureaucrats anticipate the actual elimination of milspecs and standards to be. Specifically, this chapter compares beliefs about what makes reform hard or easy between those employees who think it will be easy and those who think it will be hard. Once again, this comparison should help us to better understand how perceptions of control differ and why behavior may vary among elements of the Army acquisition work force.

Chapter Ten examines how different training programs affect the underlying subfactors analyzed in Chapters Seven, Eight, and Nine. Specifically, it examines whether or not employees who have been trained have different underlying subfactors than those who have not been trained, thus identifying the role and usefulness of training in changing employee reform behavior.

Finally, Chapter Eleven draws on the information revealed in Chapters Six through Ten to develop a comprehensive set of recommendations on how the implementation of milspec and standard reform can be improved to better motivate employees to engage in reform behavior.

The appendix presents the analytic methods used to apply the theory of planned behavior to the data collected in this study. A form of causal modeling known as Structural Equations Modeling (SEM)/Latent Variable Modeling (LVM) is employed.

Chapter Two

THE POLICY ENVIRONMENT

Which statement best reflects your feelings?

The Federal Government is inefficient and needs to undergo
the same kind of dramatic restructuring and downsizing that
is taking place in the private sector 44%

The Federal Government has some problems but mainly
needs fine tuning to make it more flexible, accountable and
user-friendly 49%

The Federal Government basically performs well 6%

Not sure 1%

—Business Week/Harris Poll in *Business Week*

[Reinvention is] about replacing large, centralized, command-and-
control bureaucracies with a very different model: decentralized,
entrepreneurial organizations that are driven by competition and
accountable to customers for the results they deliver.

—David Osborne, interviewed in *Harvard Business Review*

PUBLIC-SECTOR REFORM EFFORTS

Poll results such as those above are fueling current efforts to reform
government in the manner described by Osborne. Reinventing government, as the broader reform effort has come to be known, is
debated on both sides of the aisle in Congress, in numerous state
legislatures, and by the White House. Reinvention calls for a

reassessment of public management and service delivery with an eye toward improving efficiency and economy in the public sector. It is often hoped that this efficiency will be gained by using private-sector management techniques. Using such techniques is not new, however, and was a major theme of civil service reform efforts during the Reagan Administration. While not necessarily the only source of efforts for reforming the Army acquisition system, the current policy environment in Washington has definitely contributed to favorable trends toward acquisition reform.

The Shifting Paradigm of Public Administration

Current concerns over the cost of government services, and the potential for waste in their provision, have increased the importance of efficiency for government officials and the public. But in many respects the shift to managing for efficiency in the public sector requires the elimination of rules and procedures put in place to assure fairness and equity in public administration.

A case in point is public acquisition and procurement. Many aspects of the government procurement system are complicated and burdensome compared to the contracting/supply relationships of private-sector firms. Elements of the federal acquisition procedures, such as detailed product specifications, government standards, open and fair competition, recompetition, and even federal procurement laws, differ markedly from private practice. They could potentially increase the cost of goods procured by the government and the cost of providing goods to the government. Procurement was a major focus of Vice President Gore's National Performance Review (NPR), which emphasized simplifying a complicated and burdensome process. While some of these inefficiencies are the result of poor management or outdated procedures, some are probably the price of an equitable process. Indeed, most of these features are the result of efforts to assure fair access to federal procurement contracts and to control fraud, abuse, and graft within the process.

The Role of Empowerment

With the focus on increasing government efficiency, emphasis has also been placed on empowering public officials to make judgments outside the formal rules and procedures common in a bureaucracy—to exercise the common sense that many feel is lacking in bureaucracy today. As in the private sector, efforts to reinvent government focus heavily on providing bureaucrats with more discretion to make decisions and to be entrepreneurial. It is commonly perceived that current bureaucratic structures limit the ability, opportunity, and incentives necessary for risk-taking and innovative behavior on the part of government employees, and that such risk-taking behavior will improve the effectiveness and efficiency of government bureaucracies. Besides major reductions in the size of the bureaucracy, the recently completed NPR emphasized the need for a reduction in red tape and the empowerment of federal employees. To make such empowerment of federal employees a reality, major changes will be required in the structures, rules and procedures, and cultures of public agencies that were not designed to provide entrepreneurial or empowered bureaucratic behavior. More important, perhaps, major changes will be required in the mindsets of bureaucrats.

ACQUISITION REFORM IN THE DEPARTMENT OF DEFENSE

One of the largest federal agencies and the largest federal purchaser of goods and services is the Department of Defense (DoD). Its size, role in the economy, and reputation (fair or unfair) as a source of government waste and abuse make DoD an obvious target for reinvention. Indeed, efforts to apply private-sector remedies to bureaucratic ills have taken hold at DoD. Under past and current leadership, DoD is moving to commercialize its operations and to empower its employees, particularly in the area of defense procurement.

The most recent effort to reform defense procurement focuses on lowering costs both for the government and its contractors, rather than simply emphasizing the prevention of fraud, abuse, and mismanagement as with previous reform efforts. In addition, this round of reform emphasizes efficiency, seeking to reengineer internal processes and relationships underlying the existing acquisition systems of the DoD and the military services: the Air Force, Army, and Navy/Marine Corps (hereafter referred to as the services). In many respects the current DoD reforms seek to mirror efforts to reinvent government, and they push for the application of new private-sector-like management reforms.

A variety of initiatives and reforms are under way within DoD. The one addressed in this study concerns the perceived need to unfetter the acquisition system from excessive rules, regulations, and requirements. Specifically, it calls for the discontinuation of the use of military-unique specifications and standards in acquisition and procurement. These specifications and standards are a major element of the DoD procurement process. Specifications generally refer to products and their desired performance attributes; standards generally refer to processes and techniques used to construct/build products to specification. In short, they tell DoD contractors what products to build, and in many cases how to build them.

Defense-unique military specifications (milspecs) and standards are commonly viewed as onerous, complex, costly, and in some instances outdated. To shore up its industrial base with traditionally commercial firms and gain access to their advanced technologies, DoD elected to try to make it easier to engage in the defense business. Toward this goal, the 1994 report *Blueprint for Change: Toward a National Production Base* calls for the elimination of military specifications and standards in defense acquisition: that is, greater use of performance specifications defining a product based on its performance requirements and less use of how-to specifications telling a contractor which materials, process, and so on must be used in providing a good or service.

This is a major change for a system that has been built on rigid milspecs and standards designed to assure quality and performance. Indeed, by early 1995, Army leadership began expressing concerns that the motivations, incentives, and objectives of personnel in the field may not coincide fully with the objectives of the reforms. As one example, even though program offices were directed to eliminate milspecs and standards from all requests for proposals (RFPs) and statements of work (SOWs) on new Army contracts, RFPs and SOWs were still being written with milspecs and standards included. To monitor compliance, Army leaders had to "scrub" new RFPs to assure that elimination was taking place. This resistance from the field was anticipated, and it underlies the Army's decision to make the elimination of milspecs and standards mandatory on all new con-

tracts. Contrary to the earlier reforms, a waiver must now be re-
quested to include a milspec or standard in an RFP or SOW.

Eliminating milspecs and standards from Army acquisition relies to a
great extent on the concept of empowerment. Without milspecs and
standards, individual Army employees will now need to determine
the form, fit, and function of the products they buy. In addition,
Army personnel will now be required to determine if a product meets
performance specifications rather than milspecs and standards.
More discretion will be required in determining which suppliers and
which products are eligible for consideration in procurement contracts. Finally, employees are more empowered in their role in
defining acceptable requirements for contractors and in writing
these requirements into contracts. Changes such as these, in the
Army and the entire federal bureaucracy, will be difficult.

PUBLIC- VERSUS PRIVATE-SECTOR CONSIDERATIONS

The Army's concerns about its ability to carry out reform are not
unique—questions abound as to whether bureaucracies can or
should be reinvented. While the application of private-sector management techniques to the public sector may seem straightforward
on the surface, many observers note that differences between the
private and public sectors may complicate this process.

Managerial Constraints

Assuring equity and fairness in the management of public affairs is a
major objective for public-sector managers and has been accomplished through two primary means: (1) legal regulation of public
managers and (2) direct public accountability and control of public
administration. Many laws, such as those in the acquisition and procurement area, are directed at controlling the decisions of public
managers. Reforms that emphasize greater discretion and
"entrepreneurship" from public officials often fail to recognize that
public managers may have very real concerns that they will be prose-
cuted for violating legal requirements. The legal environment faced
by public managers, combined with the emphasis on public
accountability, makes for a very risk-averse bureaucracy.
Establishing entrepreneurship—a major goal of reinvention—in such

an environment will be hard without some change in the legal and/or political environment within which public managers operate.

Micromanagement

Moving toward greater entrepreneurship in public management is also complicated by micromanagement from Congress and other actors. While corporate boards are sometimes thought to meddle in management decisions, such meddling by Congress in activities of public-sector managers is quite normal. Besides a few self-funded government "corporations," public agencies are funded from the public purse through the annual congressional budget process. Congress authorizes and appropriates the operating and programmatic funds of government agencies. Beyond just allocating funds, committees of Congress have increasingly directed how the funds are to be managed and spent. Micromanagement of agency operations can also take place through the executive branch, which proposes the budgets of its various agencies. Although in many respects the external funding of public activities represents another aspect of public accountability, it is the micromanagement often accompanying the annual appropriation that can frustrate reform efforts. Politics can further complicate reform, since most federal agencies are run by political appointees. These appointees are highly transitory, often not even lasting out the administration that appointed them.

Bureaucratic Self-Interest

Another factor that may contribute to difficulties in implementing change is bureaucratic self-interest. Bureaucrats may resist change efforts out of pure self-interest if the changes threaten their work environment or their compensation, or require them to learn new skills. As Peter Drucker has noted, the failure of change efforts is often attributed to bureaucratic resistance. What causes this resistance, or more specifically, what explains bureaucratic behavior? In large part, resistance can be seen either as the product of the system of managing in the public sector with all its constraints, micromanagement, and political factors, or as the result of self-interested behavior from bureaucrats.

Chapter Three

THEORIES OF BUREAUCRATIC BEHAVIOR

Bureaucracy is not the simple uniform phenomenon it is
sometimes made out to be. Reality often does not
conform to scholarly theories or popular prejudices.

—James Q. Wilson, *Bureaucracy*

I do not rule Russia; ten thousand clerks do.

—Nicholas I
Quoted in Gordon Tullock, *The Politics of Bureaucracy*

This chapter outlines two basic theoretical approaches to understanding bureaucratic motives and actions. The first theory explains
bureaucracy through the rational decisions of individual bureaucrats, and it is derived from economic and organizational perspectives on bureaucracy. The second explains bureaucracy from an
institutional perspective based on the internal and external organizational factors that affect behavior, and it is commonly found in the
organizational, public administration, and political science litera-
tures. These theories provide a base for the development of a model
of bureaucratic behavior in the next chapter. Understanding theories of bureaucracy will allow us to critically examine the Army
bureaucracy—determining the extent to which it conforms or di-
verges from these theories.

THEORETICAL APPROACH ONE: SELF-INTEREST

To understand the behavior of an entire bureaucracy, many scholars have focused on the behavior of individual bureaucrats. These bureaucrats are seen as boundedly rational individuals making decisions based on self-interest maximization in a complex professional environment. Conceptualizing bureaucrats as individuals who base decisions on their perceived self-interests has led to a series of ever more complex hypotheses on what these self-interests are, what exactly bureaucrats seek to maximize, and how this affects bureaucracies and their behavior. Within these theoretical approaches, self-interest and the goals that make it up vary depending on where the bureaucrat sits within the organization, and what personal characterstics he or she brings to the job.

The Budget-Maximizing Bureaucrat

Extending the self-interest perspective on bureaucratic behavior, others have theorized that bureaucrats seek to maximize their agency's discretionary budgets. While agreeing that bureaucrats hold a variety of personal goals, each of these goals is attainable through increasing the agency's discretionary budget. Thus, it is in the bureaucrat's self-interest to work toward budget maximization. It is assumed that by doing so the bureaucrat will be able to attain a variety of subsidiary goals, such as increasing salary, perquisites, reputation, power, patronage, productivity, convenience, and ease of management (Niskanen, 1991).

This budget-maximizing perspective applies to agency executives or senior bureaucrats; it does not attempt to define or predict the behavior of lower-level bureaucrats. The central assumption is that employees at the higher levels of a bureaucracy value relatively more the organizational goals for which they are more or less directly responsible. The variation in goals and defined self-interest across the organization highlights a central aspect of all the self-interest-based theories—divergent interests and their effects on the bureaucratic organization.

Examining Divergent Interests

At the center of the self-interest approach to bureaucratic behavior is the conflict between the personal goals of bureaucrats and the goals of the organization they serve. To the extent that individual bureaucrats share the goals and objectives of the organization, an agency can expect its employees to act in a manner consistent with those objectives. When personal and organizational goals coincide, the organization is likely to be more efficient—experiencing less shirking and non-value-added activity.

Differences in these factors—goals, uncertainty, perceptions, and information—are most likely to be found between upper- and lower-level members of an organization. Once at the top of an organization, bureaucrats are likely to find themselves more directly responsible for agency outcomes—thus their interests and likely their perceptions of reality can be expected to coincide more with the organization. In addition, senior managers have more information on agency goals, objectives, and plans. This information lowers the amount of uncertainty they face—lessening divergent interests.

There is greater conflict and goal divergence within the lower ranks of a bureaucracy because this is where working bureaucrats must reconcile organizational rules with the realities of service delivery and their operating environment. The lower-level workers are more or less separated from organizational objectives. So in some types of agencies, at the bottom of the organization, objectives can appear more abstract and the rules protecting them less applicable, thus allowing greater bureaucrat discretion and greater goal divergence.

Organizations can be classified based on the observability (usually to agency managers) of their outputs and outcomes (Wilson, 1989). Outputs are the things an agency or its employees do to achieve organizational goals or satisfy the agency's mission. In bureaucracies—and public agencies in particular—outputs, outcomes, or both may be unobservable (or difficult to observe) for agency managers. In these situations, agencies or their managers tend to control bureaucratic activity to assure that agency output and outcome goals are achieved. Using Army acquisition as an example, the Army desires effective and reliable weapon systems for use in warfare; this outcome is very hard to observe during peacetime. Army managers can, however, control the process through which weapons are procured and lay out specific regulations for testing quality and reliability. These outputs include factors such as contracts awarded, milspecs and standards employed and enforced, and the number of tests conducted. Army acquisition is thus an example of observable outputs with a less than fully observable outcome.

Unobservability of agency outputs and outcomes—and the uncertainty that results for agency managers—contributes to creating procedural and process-oriented organizations. These organizations rapidly become regulated, rule-bound, and dominated by standard operating procedures.

Control, Compliance, and the Principal-Agent Framework

Self-interest explanations of bureaucratic behavior ultimately lead to the development of ways to better assure the overlap of personal and organizational interests. Divergent goals imply that maintaining control of bureaucratic behavior will be a significant problem within some bureaucracies. This issue lies at the heart of this research effort. Recognizing the potential for self-interested behavior on the part of employees and the tendency for public bureaucracies to become procedural or process-oriented, agencies must assure appropriate behavior by structuring contracts, rules, incentives, and regulations to elicit desired behavior.

THEORETICAL APPROACH TWO: INSTITUTIONAL RULES AND CONSTRAINTS

Some scholars attribute bureaucratic behavior to the institutional, organizational, and environmental context that bureaucrats operate in, rather than to their self-interest-determined behavior. These theories present a view that situational constraints—such as bureau rules, and external oversight and control—dictate behavior. These situational constraints are broadly defined as rules, or any formal or informal guidelines, controls, or constraints that dictate or influence behavior. For the purposes of this research, rules can be broken down into three broad categories: internal controls, external controls, and social controls that are commonly associated with public agencies.

Internal Controls

Internal controls are put in place by the institution or organization to control or influence the behavior of employees. They include:

- Internal regulations and standard operating procedures, which are at times legally binding and can have a major impact on how work is conducted and how bureaucrats behave;

- Facilitating policies, which are often human resources policies designed to educate, train, and motivate employees to perform desired behaviors; and

- Organizational culture, which can develop around how those goals are to be attained.

External Controls

Many of the constraints that are now an integral part of an agency's operating environment are externally generated. There are basically three categories of external control:

- Laws and regulations imposed by Congress on the conduct of public management, which constrain and affect bureaucratic behavior;

- Congressional controls on agency budgets, which can affect the behavior of an organization by either constraining or facilitating its ability to fulfill its mission; and

- The Civil Service system of rigid hierarchical controls, which provides the framework within which the bureaucracy is recruited, trained, promoted, and managed.

Social Controls

Social controls can be both internally and externally derived. Unlike the internal and external controls described above, social controls are driven by social relationships and networks and form two distinct categories:

- Social norms (professional and peer group), and

- Interest group pressures.

Social norms include peer approval, loyalty, and professional standards in determining behavior. In cases where there are conflicting organizational goals or a vague mission, bureaucratic behavior may be dictated largely by what is acceptable to key social and peer groupings within the organization. In reality, interest group pressures that affect a bureau may be reduced to Congress and the public. A common theme in the public administration literature is agency capture by an interest group. A "captured" agency will be heavily influenced by its primary interest groups.

A COMBINED FRAMEWORK FOR EXPLAINING BUREAUCRATIC BEHAVIOR

Both of the theoretical approaches described above have some appeal in explaining bureaucratic behavior. While the self-interest approach acknowledges the presence and need for constraints, it implicitly assumes that these constraints are not binding. This situation allows self-interest to be the dominant determinant of behavior. The institutional approach, on the other hand, places much greater emphasis on the power and efficacy of these constraints in controlling behavior. Thus, it implies that rules and routines have been effectively substituted for individual choice and discretion.

As Wilson's quote at the start of this chapter suggests, the issue of bureaucracy is very complex. Various theories have been proposed to explain bureaucratic behavior. By examining the bureaucratic response to reform within the Army acquisition system, we will be better able to assess these complex relationships.

Chapter Four
EXPLAINING BUREAUCRATIC BEHAVIOR

[M]anagement must pay attention to what goes on in people's heads as
well as what happens on their desks.

—Michael Hammer and James Champy,
Reengineering the Corporation: A Manifesto for Business Revolution

Human beings will behave as they are rewarded for behaving—whether
the reward be money and promotion, a medal, an autographed picture
of the boss, or a pat on the back. This is one lesson the behavioral
psychologist has taught us during the last 50 years.

—Peter F. Drucker, in *Public Interest*

To understand "what goes on in people's heads"—specifically Army
bureaucrats' heads, this study employs a model from the field of
social psychology—the theory of planned behavior (TPB) (Ajzen,
1991). This model, traditionally used to explain and predict individual volitional behaviors, provides a useful framework for determining
the factors important to bureaucratic behavior, and it provides a
mechanism for testing the various propositions about bureaucratic
behavior previously identified.

The TPB, which is represented graphically in Figure 4.1, postulates
that an individual's behavior results first from the intention to perform a given behavior. This intention is in turn caused by three central factors: (1) attitudes toward the behavior; (2) subjective norms,
or the perceptions an individual has about the normative beliefs of

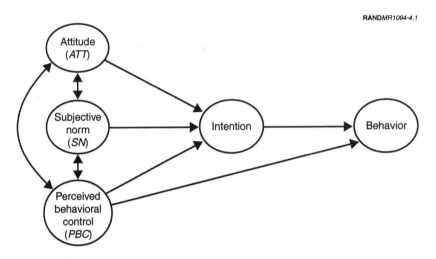

SOURCE: Ajzen (1991).

Figure 4.1—The Theory of Planned Behavior

others related to the behavior; and (3) perceived behavioral controls, or the factors believed to be constraining or facilitating an individual's behavior (Ajzen, 1991). In other words, the TPB will be used to analyze the relative effect of attitudes, subjective norms, and perceived behavioral controls on the behavior of Army bureaucrats—specifically their behavior with respect to the elimination of milspecs and standards—and will help to determine whether self-interest, rules, or some combination can actually be linked to reform behavior.

LINKING THEORY TO REALITY

The TPB model posits that three factors directly affect behavioral intentions, and thus indirectly affect behavior. These factors are attitude, subjective norm, and perceived behavioral control.

Attitude

In this study, attitude is determined by the costs and benefits perceived by a bureaucrat to result from eliminating milspecs and standards. Attitude can be measured in two ways in behavioral research, and both measures are used in this study. The first is through a global measure of attitude, such as a single-survey item asking respondents to indicate whether they have a positive or negative attitude toward performing a certain behavior. The second measure of attitude is constructed by summing the products of outcome evaluations and outcome beliefs for all possible (or measurable) outcomes involved in attitude formation. This is termed a belief-based measure of attitude, and it will be represented in this study by the symbol *ATT*. Since such an assessment of all possible outcomes is virtually impossible, this form of measurement is considered less reliable than the global attitude measure. Nevertheless, TPB researchers often measure attitude using both approaches. The two measurements are then correlated to determine how closely related they are. If this correlation is perfect (i.e., equal to one) then both measures are judged to be interchangeable and reliable.

Global attitude measures and *ATT* measures will be used to operationalize the role of self-interest in determining bureaucratic decisions. Underlying outcome beliefs and outcome evaluations are the components of the self-interest calculations of bureaucrats. Bureaucrats will tend to have a positive attitude toward reform if their self-interests are served and reform leads to a perceived positive outcome, and a negative attitude if it leads to a negative outcome.

Subjective Norms

Subjective norm is a function of a respondent's beliefs about the normative views and wishes of referents about his/her behavior, and each respondent's motivation to comply with the views and wishes of each particular referent. The term "referent" is used in this study as a general description of other individuals or groups who may have an effect on a bureaucrat's (survey respondent's) decisions or actions. Referents might include peers, colleagues, family, and professional associations—any person or group to which a bureaucrat may refer in making a decision or deciding on a behavior.

As with attitude, subjective norm is often measured in two ways in behavioral research, and both measures are used in this study. The first is a global measure of subjective norm, such as a single-survey item asking respondents to indicate whether referents important to them desire them to perform a certain behavior. The second measure of subjective norm is constructed by summing the products of normative belief and motivation to comply for all possible referents involved in subjective norm formation. This is often termed a belief-based measure of subjective norm, and it will be indicated in this study by the symbol *SN*. Again, since identification of all possible referents and measurement of associated normative beliefs and motivations is impossible to do in practice, this form of measurement is considered less reliable than the global subjective norm measure. Nevertheless, TPB researchers often measure subjective norm using both approaches. These measurements are then correlated to determine how closely related they are. If this correlation is perfect (i.e., equal to one) then both measures are judged to be interchangeable and reliable.

Subjective norm is used to operationalize the portion of the institutional rules theory of bureaucracy that identifies hierarchy, social norms, and interest group pressures as important determinants of bureaucratic behavior. Hierarchy relates to the impact on behavior of the role of superiors and position in the bureaucracy. Social norms refer to the effect of co-workers/peers and professional interests on behavior. Interest group pressure relates to the effect of external actors—Congress, the public, and others with a stake in a bureaucrat's actions—on behavior. Each of these function as types of social normative control on the bureaucrat's behavior.

Perceived Behavioral Control

The perceived behavioral control factor measures the effect of rules, regulations, and other imposed constraints that can control a bureaucrat's behavior. As with attitude and subjective norm, there are two methods of measuring perceived behavioral control that are used in applying and analyzing behavior with the TPB model. The first is a global measure of perceived behavioral control, based on a single-survey item that asks individuals if performing a certain behavior will be hard or easy for them personally. The second measure is the belief-based measure of perceived behavioral control, identified in this study by the symbol *PBC*. This measure is the summation of all possible control beliefs, and, as with the other belief-based measures, the reliability of *PBC* is affected by the difficulty in measuring control beliefs related to all measurable control factors. But if the global measure of perceived behavioral control is highly correlated with *PBC,* TPB researchers will use the information on control beliefs to better understand why and how perceptions of behavioral control differ within the population.

Clearly, the TPB is a useful means of operationalizing the constructs included in the theories surveyed previously on bureaucracy and bureaucratic behavior. The attitude factor in the TPB is developed by assessing the personal and professional consequences of reform behavior on the respondent. Thus, it is a useful factor to operationalize the self-interest construct—both for bureaucrats who are personally motivated or for those motivated to meet organizational goals. The effects of referents are operationalized through the subjective norm factor. The role of rules or other factors that constrain or facilitate behavior is effectively operationalized by the perceived behavioral control factor and to a degree by subjective norm. To make these assessments as well as test the model, data were collected from the Army acquisition work force. The collection methods used are described in the next chapter.

Chapter Five

DATA COLLECTION

A multimethod approach was used to gather the data for this report, including both qualitative data methods (interviews) and the collection of data for quantitative analysis (a comprehensive survey).

This chapter begins by describing the methods used to design and conduct the interviews of Army acquisition personnel, including a description of the relevant outcomes, referents, and controls identified through the interview process. These outcomes, referents, and controls are used to build the survey items used to collect the data in the survey stage. The design and application of the survey are described in the latter portion of the chapter.

FIELD INTERVIEW PROCESS

Construction of the belief-based measures—*ATT, SN,* and *PBC*—first requires identification of important or relevant outcomes, referents, and control factors. This identification was based on interviews conducted with employees in the Army's acquisition system, including Army, other government, and defense contractor personnel. There were three objectives for these interviews:

- To develop a better understanding of the Army acquisition system, its organization, and its personnel;

- To gather preliminary data on the extent of reform acceptance and reform-related behavior within the Army; and

- To identify relevant outcomes, referents, and controls related to the elimination of milspecs and standards that could affect acceptance of the reforms within the Army bureaucracy.

In 1995 and early 1996, 85 interviews were conducted with acquisition personnel in nine Army program offices. Interviewees were selected in the following way. A list of all Army acquisition programs that had recently written or were preparing to write a Request for Proposal (RFP) under the new acquisition reforms was prepared. Programs were selected from the following categories to assure a wide sample of perspectives across Army organizations, phase of program, and technology:

- **Program Executive Office (PEO)–managed programs.** At least one program from each of the six PEO fields was selected. In 1996 the PEO fields were Field Artillery Systems; Armored System Modernization; Aviation; Combat Support; Command, Control, and Communications; Missile Defense; Intelligence and Electronic Warfare; and Tactical Missiles.

- **Buying command.** At least one program from each of the six major buying commands was selected. In 1996 the major buying commands were Army Materiel Command (AMC) Headquarters; Aviation and Troop Command; Communications and Electronics Command; Missile Command; Simulation and Training Command; and Tank Automotive Command. In addition, the Army Research and Development Center at Picatinny Arsenal in New Jersey was included as a separate buying command, although it is not officially a major buying command.

- **Program phase.** Programs in each phase of acquisition were selected. A simplified listing of the five major program phases used to describe the acquisition process in 1996 is concept definition; demonstration and validation; engineering and manufacturing development; production and deployment; and operations and support.

- **Technology.** Programs embodying both military-unique and nondevelopmental item (NDI) or commercial, off-the-shelf technologies were selected.

Within each program selected, a range of personnel types were interviewed. Interviewees within each program were selected based on criteria designed to maximize the personal perspectives of employees. Interviewees were selected to cross career fields and seniority levels. Specifically, efforts were made to interview personnel in the following categories:

- **Career field** (including program management, engineering, software engineering, logistics, quality assurance, business management, contracting, and safety functions) to provide the perspectives of various functional and organizational affiliations;

- **Senior personnel** (including project managers and division chiefs) to provide the views of senior managers;

- **Middle management** (including deputy program managers and branch chiefs) to provide a middle-manager perspective;

- **Line staff** (working-level staff in fields such as engineering, logistics, quality assurance, and contracting) to provide the perspective of the rank-and-file acquisition employee.

Interviews, with two exceptions, were conducted by a team of two RAND researchers either two-on-one (RAND-on-Army staff) or two-on-two. A general interview protocol was used to ensure that a standard line of questioning could be maintained across interviews. This protocol is provided for the reader's reference in the appendix.

FIELD INTERVIEW RESULTS

A primary purpose of the interviews was to generate a list of relevant outcomes, referents, and controls for use in developing a survey for distribution to a wider sample of Army acquisition personnel.

Relevant Outcomes

In the interviews a set of outcomes were identified by Army acquisition personnel as relevant to the elimination of milspecs and standards. Interviewees were asked to provide their perspectives on efforts to eliminate milspecs and standards, as well as on the reform process in general. The outcomes identified can be categorized into programmatic outcomes—or those related to the weapon system or acquisition program—and personal outcomes, such as job satisfaction, workload, remuneration, etc. A total of 23 relevant outcomes were identified: 16 related to programmatic outcomes and 7 related to personal outcomes. These are listed in Table 5.1.

Based on these outcomes, corresponding survey items were developed to measure the outcome evaluations and outcome beliefs of whether a respondent thinks the outcome is desirable or undesirable and whether the outcome is likely or unlikely.

Table 5.1

Relevant Outcomes

Programmatic/ Organizational Outcomes	Personal Outcomes
• Reduce program costs	• Improve my career opportunities
• Improve project quality	• Increase the work required
• Make program management easier	• Increase my chances of getting a cash award
• Make systems less stable	• Make me responsible for problems that arise
• Reduce program delays	• Require my learning new skills
• Improve my ability to meet work objectives	• Increase my responsibilities
• Increase the chances of a contract award protest	• Reduce my authority
• Make sustainment more difficult	
• Reduce competition in the spares market	
• Increase life cycle costs	
• Increase conflict with contractors	
• Make material release harder to attain	
• Encourage commercial firms to do government work	
• Increase conflict with the "user"	
• Increase the amount of fraud in the system	
• Increase cooperation with contractors	

Relevant Referents

Based on the interviews, 19 referents—peers, superiors, and interest groups—were identified as being important to Army acquisition bureaucrats in their work place decisions. These referents are persons or groups commonly mentioned as being important in an employee's decision to eliminate milspecs and standards. They are located both internal to and external to the Army acquisition system. External referents are any interest groups outside the Army acquisition community, including upper-level DoD personnel. The referents most commonly mentioned in the interview process are shown in Table 5.2.

For each of these referents, survey items are designed to measure normative beliefs and motivations to comply: whether a respondent thinks a given referent is likely or unlikely to support milspec and standard reform and whether the referent is perceived as important or unimportant in personal work place decisions.

Table 5.2

Referent Groups Important for Determining Subjective Norm

Internal Referents	External Referents
• Secretary of the Army (ASA(ALT))	• Secretary of Defense
• Program executive officer (PEO)	• OSD staff
• Commander AMC	• Test community
• Commander of buying command	• The user
• Supervisors	• Industry
• Program/project managers	• Congress
• Co-workers	• The public
• Quality assurance personnel	
• Engineering personnel	
• Contracting personnel	
• Logistics personnel	
• Configuration management personnel	

Relevant Controls

Respondents to the interviews identified the impact of rules and regulations on their reform behavior. Based on this information a list of relevant control factors—factors that were viewed as preventing or facilitating the elimination of milspecs and standards—was compiled. This list is shown in Table 5.3.

THE ARMY ACQUISITION SURVEY

The information about relevant outcomes, referents, and control factors identified in the interview process was used to construct an original survey for distribution to a larger and broader sample of respondents. This survey was designed and used as the primary data-collection method of this study. It was designed specifically to measure the factors included in the TPB model, including reform behavior, reform intention, attitude, subjective norm, and perceived behavioral control. In the case of attitudes, subjective norms, and perceived behavioral controls, both global and belief-based measures of each factor are derived from the survey. Some items are designed to measure global factors. Belief-based measures require multiple items. Two survey items are required for each outcome or referent: outcome beliefs and evaluations, and normative beliefs and motivations to comply, respectively. For each control factor, a control belief must be measured.

Table 5.3

Salient Controls

Policy Factors	Rules and External Factors
• Training provided	• Federal acquisition laws
• Information on implementing reforms	• Army rules and regulations
• Information on working without milspecs and standards	• Standard operating procedures
• Discretion provided	• Amount of time available
	• Human resources available
	• Funds available
	• Skills of others

The survey contained 118 items in four sections. The first section was used for global measures of reform behavior and reform intention. In this section, respondents were asked to indicate the extent to which they had discontinued using milspecs and standards and the extent to which they supported the policy and intended to continue to comply with it. The second section asked questions used to derive global and belief-based measures of attitude toward reform. This included questions about outcome evaluations and outcome beliefs related to the 23 outcomes shown in Table 5.1. The third section asked questions used to derive global and belief-based measures of subjective norms toward reform. This included questions about normative beliefs and motivations to comply related to the 19 referents shown in Table 5.2. The final section measured global perceived behavioral control and the components of reform *PBC*: underlying control beliefs related to the 11 control factors listed in Table 5.3.

The overall response rate for the Army Acquisition Survey was 59 percent. The majority of responses were received after an initial mailing: 47 percent (1,412 responses). An additional 12 percent (362 responses) were received after the follow-up mailing. Overall, the response rate was fairly uniform across career groups, ranging from 57 percent for contracting personnel to 63 percent for military personnel. The uniform response rate suggests that no single group dominated the survey responses.

Chapter Six

UNDERSTANDING REFORM BEHAVIOR

This chapter addresses three sets of questions:

- What is the current state of support for reform within the acquisition work force? Are employees acting in accordance with milspec and standard reform, i.e., are they behaving as desired by Army leadership?

- How well do the data collected from the acquisition work force fit the TPB model of bureaucratic behavior discussed in Chapter Four? Is the TPB model able to predict reform behavior within the work force, and what can it tell us about which factors are important in determining behavior?

- Do the attitudes, subjective norms, and perceived behavioral controls vary in any systematic way across the acquisition work force (as might be suggested by bureaucratic theory)?

ASSESSING SUPPORT FOR MILSPEC AND STANDARD REFORM AND REFORM BEHAVIOR

A primary objective of this study is to assess the degree to which milspec and standard reform is supported and implemented by the Army acquisition work force.

In the Army Acquisition Survey, two specific items were included related to (1) the level of support a respondent felt toward the policy to eliminate all use of milspecs and standards and (2) the degree to which a respondent had eliminated milspecs and standards from use in RFPs, SOWs, and contracts (a measure of behavior). Examining responses to these items allows an assessment of overall levels of support and behavior within the work force. They also allow for assessment of the relationship between support and behavior, and its implications for the modeling approach pursued in this study.

Respondents to the survey were asked to indicate the extent to which they agreed or disagreed with the following statement: "I support the elimination of milspecs and standards." The majority of respondents (66 percent) supported the reform, and only 34 percent of the respondents did not support the reform. To measure reform behavior, respondents were asked to indicate the extent to which they agreed or disagreed with the following statement: "I no longer use milspecs and standards in my job." Similar to support levels, the majority (approximately 65 percent) of the respondents agreed that they had eliminated the use of milspecs and standards.

With regard to the relationship between support and behavior, while supporters are more likely to comply with the reform than not, support is not the only factor affecting behavior. This is consistent with the theory of planned behavior, which includes the concept of support (i.e., the attitude factor) as only one of the factors that ultimately determine intentions and behavior; subjective norms and perceived behavioral control are the others. While the work force may be "supportive" of reform, high support levels may not translate readily into the desired reform behavior.

PREDICTING REFORM BEHAVIOR

How well do the data gathered from the Army acquisition work force on milspec and standard elimination fit the theory of planned behavior? What can this model tell us about the factors important in determining bureaucratic behavior? To answer these questions, the theory of planned behavior is applied to the survey data using a form of causal modeling known as Structural Equations Modeling (SEM)/Latent Variable Modeling (LVM). This modeling and the accompanying analysis are described in detail in the appendix.

In sum, the TPB model of bureaucratic behavior used here appears to fit the data well. An employee's elimination of milspecs and standards can be predicted by that employee's intention to eliminate milspecs and standards and his/her perception of control over this behavior. In addition, the model shows that the reform intention is in turn predicted by an employee's attitude and subjective norm toward eliminating milspecs and standards.

Starting with the TPB model's exogenous factors (attitude, subjective norm, and perceived behavioral control) attitude and subjective norm affect the level of intentions. Perceived behavioral control, while posited in the general model to directly affect both reform intentions and behavior, is estimated here to have a direct effect only on behavior. In predicting intentions, attitude is the largest factor. Its effect on intentions is almost three times as large as that of subjective norm. In predicting reform behavior, both intentions and perceived behavioral control have sizable effects. Intentions have a slightly larger effect on behavior than perceived behavioral control.

The implications of the model are that efforts to promote reform behavior within the work force should focus on increasing reform intentions. This is accomplished by changing attitude and subjective norm. In addition, behavior is affected by perceived behavioral control. Acquisition personnel are more likely to behave in accordance with reform if they feel the institutions and the environment facilitate the elimination of milspecs and standards.

SUBSTANTIATING THEORIES OF BUREAUCRATIC BEHAVIOR

As discussed previously, attitude, subjective norm, and perceived behavioral control have a rough correspondence to major theoretical explanations of bureaucratic behavior. In essence, these theories on bureaucracy posit that bureaucratic behavior is primarily the result of either self-interest or institutional rules. According to the TPB, one's attitude toward a behavior is the result of a calculation of the costs and benefits of a behavior. Therefore, attitude corresponds to self-interest. Subjective norm measures the effect of referents or actors in the decision to perform a behavior. Therefore, subjective norm corresponds to the social control element of the institutional rules perspective. Finally, perceived behavioral control measures the degree to which an employee perceives environmental and organizational factors as constraining or facilitating a reform behavior.

Therefore, perceived behavioral control corresponds to the internal and external control elements of the institutional rules perspective.

The model parameter estimates derived here provide support for each of the bureaucratic theories. Each of the factors—self-interest, social controls, and the internally and externally imposed controls of the institutional rules approach—plays a significant role in predicting reform intention and reform behavior. While each factor is significant in its own right, the model provides added insight into the relative strength of each factor and how it affects behavior (either directly or indirectly through intentions).

Self-interest is a strong predictor of bureaucratic behavior through its effect on the formation of behavioral intentions. As this study shows, attitude has a strong effect on the formation of reform intentions— much larger than subjective norm (social controls) and perceived behavioral control (institutional rules). This observation lends support to the approaches to bureaucratic behavior that emphasize the role of self-interest. In general, mean attitude toward reform is positive. Given the positive relationship between attitude and reform intention in the model, this implies that the existing work force attitude is contributing to the intention to reform. It appears that the average member of the acquisition community views the ultimate outcome of milspec and standard elimination as beneficial. This positive attitude leads to an intention to eliminate milspecs and standards.

The social control aspect of institutional rules—subjective norm— also contributes to reform intentions. While less powerful than self-interest in determining intentions, the views of others (referents) are significant in the determination of reform intentions (and thus reform behavior) within the acquisition work force. Mean subjective norm for the acquisition work force is positive, implying that on average, important referents are viewed as in favor of reform. This perceived referent support for reform leads to greater reform intentions and reform behavior.

While self-interest and social controls affect reform behavior indirectly through reform intentions, the perceived effect of institutional rules—perceived behavioral control—is slightly more complicated. The model parameter estimates imply that internally and externally imposed controls do not have a statistically significant effect on reform intentions. They do, however, have a large and statistically significant direct effect on reform behavior.

While reform intention mediates the effect of self-interest and bureaucratic politics, institutional rules directly affect the ability of acquisition personnel to act on their reform intentions. The fact that mean perceived behavioral control is slightly negative reflects a perception within the work force that institutional rules make it difficult to eliminate milspecs and standards. Given the significant positive relationship between *PBC* and reform behavior, a negative perception of perceived behavioral control dampens actual reform behavior.

Perceived behavioral control has a strong positive effect on behavior. This provides direct support for the view that institutional rules affect bureaucratic behavior. In fact, the advocates of this explanation of bureaucratic behavior maintain that the purpose of rules is to directly influence behavior. The institutional rules perspective argues that institutional constraints correct for the effect of self-interest, which might divert bureaucratic behavior from what the institution wants. The model parameters support the postulated effect; however, since the value of the *PBC* measures are negative, the role of rules in this instance appears to hinder the attainment of institutional objectives rather than facilitate them. Acquisition employees tend to feel that it will be hard to implement and work without milspecs and standards; this has a negative effect on their reform behavior.

EXPLAINING DIFFERENCES IN REFORM INTENTIONS AND BEHAVIOR

As described previously, the theory of planned behavior further posits that attitude, subjective norm, and perceived behavioral control represent the summation of a set of products of underlying subfactors. These underlying subfactors are actually what determine attitude, subjective norm, and perceived behavioral control. Importantly, the results of this study indicate that attitude, subjective norm, and perceived behavioral control vary across certain dimensions, including an employee's career group, experience, organizational affiliation, and training. These differences are described in detail below.

Career Group

Results indicate that career group is an important determinant of attitude, subjective norm, and perceived behavioral control. Specifically, when compared to the military members of the acquisition work force, three civilian career groups—engineering, QA, and logistics—have significantly lower attitude, subjective norm, and perceived behavioral control values. This implies that these career groups will have less intent to eliminate milspecs and standards than military personnel and, ultimately, will exhibit less reform behavior than military personnel.

Experience Level

Results show that an employee's experience level is an important determinant of his/her attitude toward reform. Specifically, employees with over 20 years' experience on average have lower attitude scores than employees with under 20 years' experience. This lowering of attitude implies lower intention to reform, and ultimately less reform behavior.

Organizational Affiliation

Results show that an employee's organizational affiliation is an important determinant of his/her attitude and subjective norm toward reform. Employees who are affiliated with the program management (PM) office rather than the matrix are predicted to have higher attitude and subjective norm levels. Based on these results, we can expect PM personnel to have greater reform intentions and ultimately exhibit more reform behavior.

Training

Results show that jointly the three training variables have a significant effect on the level of reform attitude in the acquisition work force. Three types of training were assessed, namely traditional acquisition training, IPT-related training, and Road Show IV.

The acquisition training variable, which measures participation in any formal acquisition-related training within the Army, is not important for reform attitude, subjective norm, or perceived behavioral control. By extension, formal acquisition training does not have an important effect on an employee's intention to eliminate milspecs and standards or his actual elimination of milspecs and standards. It is important to keep in mind that formal acquisition training is not specific to milspec and standard reform. Its intent is not to cause greater reform behavior within the work force, but to train employees in acquisition management.

IPT-related training is designed to facilitate the formation and use of integrated product or process teams within the Army. Results show that participation in such training has a statistically significant effect on attitude and subjective norm: it increases them. Employees who have undergone IPT training have significantly higher attitude and subjective norm scores; thus, these employees should have greater reform intentions and exhibit more reform behavior.

Finally, participation in the Army's Road Show IV program is significantly related to higher attitude scores. Road Show IV was specifically designed to educate employees on the major reform initiatives, including milspecs and standards elimination. Results show that employees who participated in Road Show IV had a significantly more positive attitude toward eliminating milspecs and standards. This should translate into more reform intention and behavior.

To understand better why these differences in attitudes, subjective norms, and perceived behavioral control (and by extension different intentions and behavior) develop across groups, traditional TPB research examines the underlying subfactors and their differences. Furthermore, by studying how the underlying subfactors of groups differ, we can identify which subfactors need to be changed in order to give groups similar subfactors and thus, if the model is accurate, similar behaviors. The next three chapters analyze the differences in underlying subfactors that explain variation in attitude, subjective norm, and perceived behavioral control.

Chapter Seven

UNDERSTANDING REFORM ATTITUDES
WITHIN THE ACQUISITION WORK FORCE

Up to now this study has used global measures of attitude, subjective norm, and perceived behavioral control to analyze reform intention and behavior. This chapter describes how belief-based measures of attitude can be used to better explain how reform attitudes differ within the acquisition work force.

MEASURING BUREAUCRATIC ATTITUDES

There are two measures of attitude in TPB research: global attitude measures and belief-based attitude measures. Global attitude measures are single items on a survey, such as questions asking individuals if they believe a behavior is desirable or undesirable. A global attitude measure incorporates the assessment of all relevant outcome beliefs (B) and outcome evaluations (E). For this reason it is often considered to be the most reliable measure of attitude. Such measures do not, however, allow the examination of these underlying subfactors—outcome beliefs and outcome evaluations—and their role in attitude formation.

Belief-based measures of attitude do allow the examination of underlying subfactors. In the TPB, one's attitude toward a behavior is defined as one's evaluation of whether or not performing a given behavior is beneficial or harmful to one's self-interest (defined either personally, organizationally, or in some combination). Determination of whether a given behavior is beneficial or harmful results from the assessment of all the potential outcomes—good and bad—that can result from it (specifically in this study, eliminating milspecs and standards). For example, one possible outcome of milspec and stan-

41

dard reform is a reduction in program costs. Such an outcome can be more or less important to an employee depending on whether his or her self-interest is weighted toward personal or organizational goals. The assessment of such an outcome is made up of two subfactors:

- Outcome evaluation *(E)*, defined as how good or bad a potential outcome resulting from reform behavior—reduction in program costs—is assessed to be; and

- Outcome belief *(B)*, perceptions of how likely or unlikely it is that a given behavior will result in a given outcome—a reduction in program costs.

The assessment of a single outcome, and its contribution to the attitude toward a behavior, is given by the product of its outcome evaluation and outcome belief (the $B \times E$ product). Belief-based attitude is defined simply as the summation of all relevant $B \times E$ products:

$$ATT = \sum_{i=1}^{n} \left(B_i \times E_i \right).$$

ATT is the belief-based or subfactor-determined measure, and n is the number of relevant outcomes. The subscript i indexes the relevant outcomes. In this study, 23 potential outcomes of eliminating milspecs and standards were included; they are listed in Table 5.1. A limitation to this approach is that researchers must identify all relevant outcomes and measure the underlying subfactors associated with them. Since this is almost impossible to do in practice, belief-based measures are considered less reliable than global measures.

One of the advantages of the TPB model is its identification of the role of underlying subfactors in the formation of attitude, subjective norm, and perceived behavioral control—outcome evaluations and outcome beliefs in the case of attitude. Examining these underlying subfactors allows analysis of the specific concerns that are most important in determining attitude and, ultimately, behavior. Traditionally, TPB researchers use the global attitude measures to estimate and fit the TPB model to the data. This provides a test of the applicability of the TPB model to the population under study. They then compare the belief-based *(ATT)* measure with the global measures. If the two measures meet a set of comparison criteria, this implies that the underlying subfactors measured are a reliable indicator of the global measure. If the comparison criteria are met, TPB researchers will analyze and examine the underlying subfactors to get a better understanding of how the globally measured attitude is formed.

The data from the Army Acquisition Survey indicate that the global and belief-based attitude measures are comparable. Therefore, we can now examine underlying subfactors to assess where significant differences exist within the acquisition work force.

EXPLAINING DIFFERENCES IN BUREAUCRATIC REFORM ATTITUDES

Underlying outcome beliefs and evaluations are compared across career groups, experience levels, and organizational affiliations. For career groups, we compared underlying subfactors to those of military personnel. Military personnel, along with contracting personnel, have the highest mean global attitudes toward reform. For experience level, comparisons will be made to those employees with under 20 years' experience—the more supportive group when compared to those with over 20 years. For organizational affiliation, comparisons will be made to PM personnel—who are more supportive than their complement, matrix personnel.

In employing this approach we are attempting to better understand why various career groups hold different attitudes. Why do QA personnel, solely as a function of their career group, hold a lower attitude toward reform than military personnel? Analyzing the underlying subfactors, we find that the difference, resulting solely from a QA affiliation, is explained by the fact that QA personnel believe that reform is less likely to increase product quality.

Why do we care about identifying differences in underlying subfactors? These differences provide information on how groups differ (which may in itself be useful), and they also suggest which subfactors may be important in changing attitudes and, then, behavior for certain groups. The ultimate goal of policymakers is compliance with the directive to eliminate milspecs and standards from use. Having identified a group more in compliance than other groups, such as the military in the example above, we can set a benchmark for other groups. Once we know the underlying subfactors concerning reform that characterize personnel who both do and do not support reform, we have valuable information about how to target subfactors of those who do not support it. If we want less supportive groups—in this example QA personnel—to behave more like the military, we might try to raise their underlying subfactors to the same level. Knowing that the military believe product quality will improve suggests a strategy of convincing QA personnel that product quality will improve.

Five important conclusions can be drawn from the analysis. They are described below.

Differences in Outcome Beliefs Are Key

Table 7.1 shows—by career group, experience level, and organizational affiliation—where significant differences in $B \times E$ product exist for each of the 23 potential reform outcomes surveyed. For each outcome, a shaded cell indicates that there was a significant difference in the partial correlation coefficient between the $B \times E$ product and inclusion in the indicated group. In addition, each shaded cell indicates the primary source of the difference in $B \times E$ product. A "B" indicates that differences in outcome beliefs primarily caused it, an "E" signifies that differences in outcome evaluations primarily caused it, and an "E&B" signifies that differences in both outcome evaluations and beliefs were important.

Table 7.1 shows that there is at least one significant difference in the $B \times E$ product for 17 of the 23 potential outcomes. In total, there are 43 cases where the $B \times E$ products differed significantly between a given group and the base group. Of these, 30 were primarily the result of differences in outcome beliefs and 6 were due to a combination of outcome beliefs and outcome evaluations. Clearly, differences in outcome beliefs are critical to understanding differences in reform attitude (the value of the ATT measures) between the groups.

Differences in outcome beliefs are most important in explaining the differences in reform attitude for three civilian career groups: engineering, QA, and logistics. Of these three civilian career groups, the greatest number of significant $B \times E$ product differences exist

Table 7.1

Differences in Belief-Based Measures of Attitude Across Career Group, Experience Level, and Organization

Eliminating milspecs and standards will . . .	Engineering[a]	QA[a]	Logistics[a]	Contracting[a]	Over 20 Years[b]	Matrix[c]
1. Reduce program costs						E&B
2. Improve product quality	B	B	B			
3. Make program management easier	B	B				
4. Make systems less stable		B				
5. Reduce program delays	B	B				
6. Improve my career opportunities		B				
7. Improve my ability to meet work objectives	B	B	B	B		
8. Increase the work required						
9. Increase my chances of getting a cash award	E	E	E	E		
10. Make me responsible for problems that arise						
11. Increase the chance of a contract award protest						
12. Make sustainment more difficult			B		B	

[a]Comparisons relative to military personnel.

[b]Comparisons relative to under 20 years' experience.

[c]Comparisons relative to program management personnel.

$E = B \times E$ product change results from differences in outcome evaluations (E).

$B = B \times E$ product change results from differences in outcome beliefs (B).

E&B = $B \times E$ product change results from differences in both E and B.

Table 7.1—continued

Eliminating milspecs and standards will . . .	Engineering[a]	QA[a]	Logistics[a]	Contracting[a]	Over 20 Years[b]	Matrix[c]
13. Reduce competition in the spares market		B	B			
14. Increase life cycle costs	B	B	B			
15. Increase conflict with contractors		B				
16. Make material release harder to attain						
17. Encourage commercial firms to do government work	E&B	E&B	E			
18. Increase conflict with the "user"						
19. Require my learning new skills		B				
20. Increase the amount of fraud in the system	B	B				
21. Increase my responsibilities	B	B	E	E&B		
22. Reduce my authority	E&B	B	E&B	E		B
23. Increase cooperation with contractors	B	B	B			

[a]Comparisons relative to military personnel.
[b]Comparisons relative to under 20 years' experience.
[c]Comparisons relative to program management personnel.

$E = B \times E$ product change results from differences in outcome evaluations (E).

$B = B \times E$ product change results from differences in outcome beliefs (B).

E&B $= B \times E$ product change results from differences in both E and B.

between QA and military personnel: 16. Of these, 14 are the result of differences in outcome beliefs. Engineers and logisticians have significantly different $B \times E$ products on 10 outcomes each. For engineers, 7 of the 10 differences are explained by differences in outcome beliefs. For logisticians, 6 of the 10 differences are explained by differences in outcome beliefs.

In summary, the civilian career groups believe that the potential positive outcomes of reform are less likely to occur and negative outcomes more likely to occur. In particular, the civilian career groups are statistically significantly less likely to believe that reform will result in the following seven potential positive outcomes: (1) improve product quality, (2) improve abilities to meet work objectives, (3) increase cooperation with contractors, (4) increase responsibilities, (5) encourage commercial firms to do government work, (6) make program management easier, and (7) reduce program delays.

These same career groups—engineering, QA, and logistics—are also more likely to believe that reform will result in the following three potential negative outcomes: (1) increase life cycle costs, (2) reduce my authority, and (3) reduce competition in the spares market.

Nonmilitary Personnel Value Reform Outcomes Differently

In addition to differences in outcome beliefs, differences in outcome evaluations are important in explaining the difference in $B \times E$ product between the civilian career groups and the military. Specifically, differences in evaluations are important in explaining the difference in $B \times E$ product for the following two outcomes: (1) increase my chances of getting a cash award and (2) encourage commercial firms to do government work.

The evaluations of cash awards were interesting. The high valuation—indicating that they are desirable—placed on cash awards relative to military personnel drove the difference in $B \times E$ product. The civilian career groups place a much higher premium on cash awards than military personnel do. This result must be viewed with caution. Military personnel, as a general rule, do not receive cash awards and so may be expected to value them much less. However, in this case we would expect the outcome assessment of receiving a cash award to be negative for military personnel, when in fact the mean evaluation of cash awards is slightly positive (0.12). This would indicate that military personnel do place some value on an increased chance of a cash award. Civilians, however, place significantly more value on this chance.

The case of encouraging commercial firms to do government work, although one of the few instances where differences in outcome evaluations are key to explaining $B \times E$ product differences, is indicative of a broader trend within the civilian career fields. For this potential positive reform outcome, the civilian career groups have a significantly lower evaluation—they do not value greater commercial firm involvement as much as the military does.

While not indicated in Table 7.1, the partial correlation coefficients on outcome evaluations reported throughout this chapter tend to indicate that the civilian career groups value potential positive reform outcomes relatively less, and value negative reform outcomes relatively more. In other words, it appears that the civilian career groups do not value the potential benefits of reform as much as the military, but at the same time they are less averse to the potential negative outcomes.

Beliefs About Programmatic Outcomes Explain Attitude Differences

Of the 23 potential outcomes surveyed, 16 relate to programmatic outcomes—effects on the weapon system program and work conducted for the program—and 7 relate to personal outcomes—effects on personal standing or comfort.

Of the 11 outcomes identified as being differentially evaluated by civilian personnel, 8 relate to programmatic outcomes. In general there were no great differences in $B \times E$ products related to personal outcomes. For three of the seven potential personal outcomes— increase the work required (item #8), make me responsible for problems that arise (item #10), and require my learning new skills (item #19)—there is no statistically significant difference in the $B \times E$ product between the career groups, experience levels, or organizational affiliations. For an additional outcome—improve my career opportunities—only QAs differed significantly from military personnel. The three personal outcomes that were consistently evaluated differently between the civilian career groups and the military were (1) increase my chances of a cash award, (2) increase my responsibilities, and (3) reduce my authority.

Based on these results, it appears that differences in reform attitude and ultimately behavior between the civilian career groups and the military are not the result of differences in perceptions of how reform will affect personal interests, but in differences in the perceived effect of reform on programmatic outcomes and objectives: cost, schedule, and quality.

Concern over Sustainment Explains Differences in Attitude by Experience Level

As Table 7.1 shows, the $B \times E$ products for personnel with over 20 years' experience and those with under 20 years' experience differ for only one of the potential outcomes: making sustainment more difficult. Is it possible that this difference adequately explains the difference in reform attitude between these two groups? It may also be possible that differences in other, unmeasured beliefs play a role. However, based on the data collected here, these two groups differ only in their outcome beliefs related to sustainment. Basically, more experienced employees are more likely to believe that sustainment will be made more difficult as a result of reform.

Organizational Effects on Reform Attitude Explained by Differences in Subfactors Related to Program Costs and Reductions in Authority

The significantly lower attitude values for matrix personnel are related to differences in the $B \times E$ products of two outcomes: reduce program costs and reduce my authority. Reducing program costs is clearly an objective of program managers and their offices, but it appears to be less important to matrix personnel, who evaluate this outcome lower than PM personnel do. In addition, matrix personnel feel that reform is less likely to result in cost reductions than PM personnel do.

In many ways the elimination of milspecs and standards removes authority from the matrix side of the Army acquisition system. The matrix is the traditional home of milspecs and standards and their administrators. Matrix personnel are significantly more likely to believe that reform will reduce their authority, in turn lowering their $B \times E$ product for this outcome.

Chapter Eight

UNDERSTANDING SUBJECTIVE NORMS WITHIN THE ACQUISITION WORK FORCE

The intention to implement milspec reform is also affected by an individual's subjective norm. For the Army personnel surveyed, variation in subjective norm levels has been shown to be related to an employee's career group and his/her organizational affiliation. Employing the same analytic methods as Chapter Seven, this chapter examines differences in the underlying subfactors that make up subjective norm and explains why it varies across the work force, thus helping to clarify some of the variation in reform behavior.

MEASURING SUBJECTIVE NORMS OF BUREAUCRATS

There are two measures of subjective norm: the global measure and the belief-based measure (SN). The relationship between these two measures is identical to the relationship between global and belief-based measures of attitude discussed in Chapter Seven. The global measures are used to test and estimate the behavioral model because they are assumed to have greater reliability. The belief-based measures are used to analyze the role and importance of underlying subfactors in explaining variation in subjective norms between groups.

In the TPB, one's subjective norm toward a behavior is defined as one's assessment of whether or not people important to him or her feel the behavior should be performed. This assessment is conducted for a number of relevant referents (one possible referent group, for example, is co-workers). The belief-based measurement of subjective norm is composed of two subfactors:

- Normative belief *(NB)*, assessment of how likely or unlikely it is that work place referents—such as co-workers—support reform behavior; and

- Motivation to comply *(MC)*, a personal assessment of how motivated one is to comply with these same work place referents—such as co-workers.

The impact of a single referent on the subjective norm of a subject is considered to be the product of the normative belief about that referent and the motivation to comply with that referent (the $NB \times MC$ product). A positive $NB \times MC$ product indicates that combined beliefs contribute to a subjective norm (referent influence) that is supportive of reform; a negative $NB \times MC$ product indicates the opposite. An individual's belief-based subjective norm (or *SN*) toward reform behavior is defined simply as the summation of all relevant $NB \times MC$ products.

$$SN = \sum_{i=1}^{n} \left(NB_i \times MC_i \right).$$

SN is the belief-based measure of subjective norm and *n* is the number of relevant referents. The subscript *i* indexes the *NB* and *MC* for each referent surveyed. In this study, *SN* was assessed based on the 19 referents listed in Table 5.2. To use belief-based measures, they must meet the same reliability and correlation criteria as belief-based and global attitude measures.

EXPLAINING DIFFERENCES IN SUBJECTIVE NORMS WITHIN THE ACQUISITION WORK FORCE

As was done in Chapter Seven, we compare underlying subfactors to a base group. The base group selected is that group with the highest subjective norm values. In this case, these groups match those used in Chapter Seven. For career group, comparisons will be made between military personnel and all other groups. For organizational affiliation, we will compare the underlying subfactors of program management personnel to matrix personnel.

Six important conclusions can be drawn from the analysis. They are described below.

Differences in Normative Beliefs Are Important

Table 8.1 shows—by career group and organizational affiliation—where significant differences in $NB \times MC$ product exist for each of the 19 referents surveyed. For each referent, a shaded cell indicates that there was a significant difference in the partial correlation between the $NB \times MC$ product and inclusion in the indicated group. In addition, each shaded cell indicates the primary source of the difference in $NB \times MC$ product. An "NB" indicates normative beliefs primarily caused it, an "MC" indicates that differences in motivation to comply caused it, and an "NB&MC" indicates that both normative beliefs and motivation to comply were important.

Table 8.1 shows that there are significant changes in the $NB \times MC$ product associated with 15 of the 19 referents. Across the civilian career groups and for the matrix generally, there are 37 instances where the $NB \times MC$ product for a given referent differed significantly between a given group and the base group. Of these, 14 are primarily the result of differences in normative beliefs, 15 are the result of differences in normative beliefs and motivations to comply, and 6 are caused by differences in motivations to comply.

Normative beliefs, or the combination of normative beliefs and motivation to comply, determine the majority of the changes in $NB \times MC$ products. Differences in the $NB \times MC$ products were not significant across career group or organization for only four referents, including the Secretary of Defense (item #1), OSD staff (item #2), logistics management personnel (#15), and configuration management personnel (item #16).

Immediate Referents Are Viewed as Less Supportive of Reform

As Table 8.1 shows, for the three important civilian career groups and the matrix in general, significant differences in $NB \times MC$ product are

Table 8.1

Differing Belief-Based Measures of Subjective Norms Across Career Group and Organization

Work Place Referents	Engineering[a]	QA[a]	Logistics[a]	Contracting[a]	Matrix[b]
1. Secretary of Defense					
2. OSD staff					
3. ASA(ALT)	NB&MC	NB&MC	NB&MC	NB	
4. Commander AMC	MC				MC
5. Commander of buying command		NB&MC		NB&MC	MC
6. Program executive officer	NB&MC	IND	NB&MC	NB&MC	NB&MC
7. Test community		IND			
8. The "user"		NB	NB		
9. My supervisor	NB	NB	NB		NB
10. The program manager	NB&MC	NB	NB	NB&MC	NB&MC
11. My co-workers	NB	NB	NB		NB
12. Quality assurance		NB&MC			
13. Engineering		NB			
14. Contracting personnel				NB&MC	
15. Logistics management					
16. Configuration management					
17. Industry	MC				
18. Congress	MC				
19. The public	MC		NB&MC		

[a]Comparisons relative to military personnel.
[b]Comparisons relative to program management personnel.

NB = $NB \times MC$ product change results from differences in normative beliefs (NB).
MC = $NB \times MC$ product change results from differences in motivation to comply (MC).
NB&MC = $NB \times MC$ product change results from differences in both NB and MC.
IND = cause of $NB \times MC$ product change is indeterminate.

evident for immediate work place referents, such as supervisors, co-workers, and program managers. In almost all cases, these differences are the result of differences in normative beliefs—with the civilian career groups and matrix personnel tending to believe that their supervisors, co-workers, and program managers are relatively less supportive of reform.

Normative Beliefs and Motivation to Comply Related to Army Acquisition Leadership Differ by Career Group

The $NB \times MC$ products related to Army acquisition leadership—ASA(ALT) and the PEOs—differ between the three civilian career groups and military personnel. These differences are the result of differences in both normative beliefs and motivations to comply. Specifically, engineers, QAs, and logisticians tend to believe that Army leadership is less supportive of reform than military personnel do (normative beliefs). In addition, these same groups are less motivated to comply with the views of acquisition leadership compared to military personnel. Matrix personnel hold similar beliefs with respect to PEOs (as compared to PM personnel).

Normative Beliefs and Motivation to Comply Related to Matrix Leadership Differ by Organization

It is not necessarily surprising that when compared to PM personnel, matrix personnel are more motivated to comply with their organizational superiors. As Table 8.1 shows, there are significant differences in the $NB \times MC$ products for matrix leadership—Commander AMC and commander of the buying command—between matrix and PM personnel. These differences are the result of differences in motivation to comply. As discussed earlier, matrix personnel are more motivated to comply with their matrix superiors than are PM personnel.

Normative Beliefs and Motivation to Comply with Non-Army Referents Are Limited

The 19 referents surveyed can be broken into two categories: Army and non-Army. Non-Army referents include the Secretary of Defense and the OSD staff as well as external-to-DoD referents such as industry (item #17), Congress (item #18), and the public (item #19). Across career group and organizational affiliation, differences in normative beliefs and motivations to comply were relatively limited with regard to these referents. With few exceptions, the various career groups and their overarching organizations in general share the same underlying normative beliefs and motivations to comply with non-Army referents. In other words, differences in beliefs related to non-Army referents do not appear very important in explaining differences in subjective norm between the three civilian career groups and military personnel, or between matrix and PM personnel.

Users Are Viewed as Less Supportive of Reform by QA and Logistics Personnel

Two civilian career groups—QA and logistics—have statistically significantly lower $NB \times MC$ products related to users than military personnel do. This difference is the result of differences in normative beliefs between the two civilian career groups and military personnel. Compared to military personnel, QA and logistics personnel perceive the user as less supportive of milspec and standard reform.

Having examined differences in underlying subfactors for attitudes and subjective norm toward reform, all that remains is an examination of differences in control beliefs. The next chapter examines differences in control beliefs across career groups.

Chapter Nine

UNDERSTANDING PERCEIVED BEHAVIORAL CONTROL WITHIN THE ACQUISITION WORK FORCE

[S]ome of the major capabilities of modern institutions come from their effectiveness in substituting rule-bound behavior for individually autonomous behavior.

—James G. March and Johan P. Olsen,
Rediscovering Institutions: The Organizational Basis of Politics

[G]overnment management tends to be driven by the constraints on the organization, not the tasks of the organization.

—James Q. Wilson, *Bureaucracy*

As the model estimated in Chapter Six shows, perceptions of behavioral control have a direct effect on the predicted behavior of Army acquisition employees. Variation in perceived behavioral control levels has been shown to be related to an employee's career group. This chapter examines differences in the control beliefs that comprise perceived behavioral control in order to better explain why these perceptions vary across the work force. By identifying how control beliefs vary, we can better understand why aggregate perceived behavioral control varies, thus helping to explain some of the variation in reform behavior.

MEASURING PERCEIVED BEHAVIORAL CONTROL OF BUREAUCRATS

There are two measures of perceived behavioral control: the global measure and the belief-based measure *(PBC)*. The relationship between these two measures is identical to the relationship between global and belief-based measures of attitude and subjective norm discussed in Chapters Seven and Eight. We use the global measures to test and estimate the behavioral model because they are assumed to have greater reliability. We use the belief-based measures to analyze the role and importance of control beliefs in explaining variation in perceived behavioral control between groups.

In the TPB, one's perceived behavioral control with regard to reform behavior is defined as one's assessment of how hard or easy it is to carry out a given behavior. A number of factors—environmental and organizational—can make a given reform behavior easier or harder to perform. The belief-based measurement of perceived behavioral control *(PBC)* is the assessment of these various control factors, and in theory it is composed of two subfactors:

- Control belief *(C)*, assessment as to whether or not a given control factor—such as acquisition laws—makes it harder or easier to eliminate milspecs and standards; and

- Control power *(P)*, an assessment of the strength of the given control factor in actually affecting behavior.

In this study, only control beliefs are used to construct the belief-based measure of *PBC* because control power variables have yet to be operationalized effectively. The impact of a single control factor on perceptions of behavioral control is measured by the control beliefs *(C)*. An individual's belief-based measure of perceived behavioral control (or *PBC*) toward reform behavior is defined simply as the summation of control beliefs across all control factors measured, or

$$PBC = \sum_{i=1}^{n} C_i .$$

Control beliefs relate to the perceived effect of constraining and facilitating factors—such as time, funding, and regulations—on a person's reform behavior. A positive control belief indicates that a given control factor is thought to facilitate reform behavior. A negative control belief indicates that a control factor is thought to constrain reform behavior.

PBC is the belief-based measure of perceived behavioral control and *n* is the number of relevant control factors. The subscript *i* indexes the relevant control factors surveyed. In this study, *PBC* was assessed based on the 11 control factors listed in Table 5.3. To use belief-based measures, they must meet the same reliability and correlation criteria as belief-based and global attitude and subjective norm measures. The data from the Army Acquisition Survey indicate that the global and belief-based subjective norm measures are comparable.

EXAMINING DIFFERENCES IN PERCEIVED BEHAVIORAL CONTROL WITHIN THE ACQUISITION WORK FORCE

As was done in Chapters Seven and Eight, underlying subfactors—in this case, control beliefs—are compared to a base group. The base group selected is that group with the highest perceived behavioral control values. As in previous chapters, career group comparisons will be made between military personnel and all other groups. While relatively straightforward, the following three conclusions emerge from the analysis.

Civilians Perceive Less Behavioral Control

Examining control beliefs in which there is a significant difference between a given career group and the military, we found that civilian career groups perceive less behavioral control than military personnel do. For the 11 control beliefs surveyed, QA and logistics personnel perceive all of them to be significantly more constraining than military personnel do. Engineers view 7 of 11 as more constraining, and contracting personnel view 5 of 11 as more constraining. As noted earlier, the global perceived behavioral control level of contracting personnel is not statistically different from that of military personnel, thus explaining the fact that they differ significantly from the military in their perceptions of only 5 of 11 control beliefs. The remaining three civilian career groups, however, differ significantly from the military on more control factors.

Civilians View Reform Policy Factors as Inadequate

Four of the 11 control factors can be described as reform policy factors. These factors are policies or initiatives undertaken within the Army acquisition system to facilitate or implement broader acquisition reform and the elimination of milspecs and standards.

The four reform policy factors are the training provided, information on how to eliminate milspecs, the discretion provided, and information on how to work without milspecs.

In all four cases, engineers, QAs, and logisticians perceive that these factors make the elimination of milspecs and standards harder (when compared to military personnel). The three civilian career groups find these reform policy factors to be inadequate, compared to the beliefs of military personnel.

Civilians View Environmental Factors as More Constraining

The remaining control factors can be described as environmental. These factors represent broader elements or conditions in the acquisition system that can affect a person's perception of the ease with which milspecs and standards can be eliminated. While these factors are variable, or changeable, to some degree, in most cases their alteration or adjustment tends be outside the control of any single actor in the system. These control factors include acquisition laws, the availability of funds, Army acquisition regulations, standard operating procedures in an office, the time available for program management, the skills of others, and the human resources available for program management.

For engineers, QAs, and logisticians, these seven factors are considered to make the elimination of milspec and standards harder rather than easier. Specifically, QAs and logisticians feel more than military personnel do that these seven factors constrain their behavior. Engineers, when compared to military personnel, find acquisition laws, Army acquisition regulations, and the time available for program management to be more constraining. Thus, besides sharing control perceptions related to the reform policy factors noted above, all three civilian career groups share the perception that acquisition laws, Army acquisition regulations, and the time provided to manage an acquisition program make it harder to eliminate milspecs and standards.

Compared to military personnel, engineers, QAs, and logisticians feel that the training and information provided on acquisition reform is relatively more constraining on their efforts to eliminate milspecs and standards. It has also been noted previously that training is related to a significantly more favorable attitude toward reform. Taking these two apparently contradictory factors into account, the next chapter examines current training programs and their effect on underlying subfactors.

Chapter Ten

ASSESSING THE ROLE OF TRAINING

We are rapidly becoming the world's smartest, most responsive buyer of best-value goods and services for our warfighter's needs. However, we sense that, due to the pressures of daily work, an emphasis on accomplishing our missions, and the sheer difficulty of communicating across our broad and diverse organization, we have not adequately communicated the changes and educated our work force on the numerous policy and procedural changes.

—Under Secretary of Defense Paul Kaminsky

Since the spring of 1992, the Army Materiel Command has traveled annually to its major subordinate commands to carry a philosophy of streamlining acquisition management to the acquisition work force. The results have been very gratifying, both in terms of the reactions of the participants and in the positive impact on material acquisition programs.

—James W. Brown (coordinator of Army Road Show training efforts), in *Acquisition Reform Today*

The success of any effort to bring behavioral change within an organization depends in part on effective communication and training efforts. This chapter examines differences in underlying subfactors between Army personnel who have received reform-related training and those who have not. Results of this study show that training has a statistically significant positive effect on reform attitude and, in some cases, subjective norm. Examination of the differences in subfactors between those with and without training can help us to better understand why attitude, subjective norm, and ultimately behavior differ between the two groups.

REFORM-RELATED TRAINING

Motivated by the Perry Initiatives, Army leadership has directed that use of milspecs and standards be discontinued, and it has also made efforts to persuade the acquisition work force that this change in policy is desirable. Specifically, the Army has made efforts to train its work force on how to eliminate milspecs and standards, as well as on how to work in an environment without milspecs and standards. Not all of the relevant training programs focus solely on the issue of eliminating milspecs and standards.

Three major training programs have been conducted that may affect an employee's intention and behavior related to eliminating milspecs and standards. Two do not focus solely on milspecs and standards. They are traditional acquisition management courses offered through the Defense Acquisition University (DAU) and Integrated Product/Process Team (IPT) training. The third program focuses on procedures for eliminating milspecs and standards: Road Show training, specifically Road Show IV training.

Traditional Acquisition Management Courses

Traditional DoD program management and acquisition courses offered through DAU may have an effect on an employee's willingness to accept and implement reform initiatives. DAU is made up of a variety of schools and centers devoted to training members of the acquisition work force. The most notable of these institutions is the Defense Systems Management College (DSMC) at Fort Belvoir, Virginia. DSMC trains current and future generations of program managers and conducts research on the acquisition system and its processes. Formal acquisition management courses at DSMC include program management, logistics management, contract management, manufacturing and production management, systems engineering management, test and evaluation management, and other areas. These courses are designed to improve an employee's knowledge of the acquisition system and the complexities of managing an acquisition program.

In this study, respondents to the survey were asked to indicate if they had ever received formal acquisition management courses through DAU.

IPT Training

A major element of the Perry Initiatives and the Army's acquisition reform efforts is the introduction and expanded use of IPTs within the acquisition process. Three types of IPTs exist within the Army. The first are overarching IPTs that are made up of Army and DoD personnel involved in acquisition management. They usually include program managers (PMs), personnel from other Army acquisition organizations, Army acquisition leadership (ASA(ALT)), and representatives of DoD acquisition oversight organizations. The second are program-level IPTs that are made up of members of the PM office and the affiliated matrix organizations. They are meant to span the various functional and professional groups involved in Army program management. The third type are contractor IPTs, which are teams made up of PM personnel and prime (or sub) contractor personnel. They are designed to bridge communication gaps between the Army and its suppliers. IPTs are meant to integrate various players in the process of managing a weapon system's acquisition. They also allow a better flow of communication and information earlier in the management process. Earlier communication is meant to improve efficiency by increasing the opportunity for various functional groups or stakeholders to exchange information and minimize risk through better information.

It is possible that IPT-related training could affect an acquisition employee's willingness to cooperate with efforts to eliminate milspecs and standards. If IPT-related training focuses on the positive attributes of teaming and the potential for reducing personal or functional risk in the acquisition process, it is possible that employees may be more willing to take the risks necessary to eliminate milspecs and standards.

Respondents to the survey were asked if they had ever participated in IPT-related courses or training sessions provided by one or more of the following four sources: (1) any DAU-affiliated institution (formal IPT training); (2) external providers, such as local colleges, universities, or training consultants; (3) contractor providers (training by a prime or subcontractor on a given Army system); and (4) internal providers (training provided by the PM, PEO, or the buying command, but not through DAU or its components).

Road Show IV Training

The Army's Road Show process is a training and communication program (headed by the Army Materiel Command) directed at the upper, middle, and lower levels of the Army acquisition system. Generally, each Road Show effort has a reform theme around which a communication effort is constructed. Road Show IV, which took place during 1994 and 1995, was dedicated to training employees about the elimination of milspecs and standards, use of IPTs, and application of best-value source selection in the acquisition process. Multiple Road Show IV programs were undertaken around the country. They were usually conducted at a major subordinate or buying command (such as CECOM in Fort Monmouth, New Jersey; ATCOM in St. Louis, Missouri; or TACOM in Detroit, Michigan).

The Road Show IV program was typically three days long and included presentations by Army leadership, along with workshops and exercises on acquisition streamlining (milspec and standard elimination, IPT use, and best-value contracting). Army leadership, starting with the Assistant Secretary of the Army (Acquisition, Logistics, and Technology) (ASA(ALT)), communicated acquisition reform goals and initiatives directly to the participants. Other workshops and exercises were designed to educate employees on the desirability of replacing milspecs and standards with performance-based specifications and other goals. These exercises also included hands-on development of RFPs and SOWs that did not require milspecs and standards.

If Road Show IV was effective, participants in the program can be expected to support reform efforts more, and to have eliminated milspecs and standards from use more, than those who did not participate in training. Survey respondents were asked directly if they had attended Road Show IV.

PARTICIPATION IN REFORM-RELATED TRAINING

Participation in the training programs just described is not universal in the Army acquisition work force (see Table 10.1). Most acquisition employees have attended traditional acquisition management courses: from 56 to 96 percent of employees in each of the five major career groups. Military personnel in the sample had the largest traditional acquisition management course experience, at 96 percent. This is not surprising, given that military personnel are commonly slotted for program management positions and training is often tailored to military personnel. More surprising is the fact that traditional acquisition course participation is lowest among engineers, at 57 percent. Engineers are the largest single career group in the acquisition system and are involved in almost every phase of the acquisition cycle.

Participation in IPT training is between 44 and 59 percent for the various career groups in the sample. Again, military personnel have the greatest experience with IPT training, at 59 percent. Contracting personnel have the lowest levels of IPT training, at 36 percent. This could be explained by the somewhat independent and legal nature of the contracting function. However, the concept of a program IPT is meant to include the contracting function.

Road Show IV, the most specific training for the elimination of milspecs and standards, is also the least common of the three types of training in the sample. Between 19 and 31 percent of the employees in the five career groups participated in Road Show IV. Participation

Table 10.1

Participation in Various Training Programs by Career Group

	Traditional Acquisition Courses	Integrated Product Team Training	Road Show IV
Engineering	57%	44%	21%
Quality assurance	64%	52%	19%
Logistics	79%	51%	20%
Contracting	81%	36%	31%
Military	96%	59%	22%

was greatest among contracting personnel—31 percent—and lowest among QA personnel. Compared to the other two training programs, participation in Road Show IV is fairly uniform at about 20 percent for each career group, except contracting.

USEFULNESS OF TRAINING IN CHANGING REFORM BEHAVIOR

What is the relationship between the various training programs and reform attitude, subjective norm, and perceived behavioral control?

In summary: (1) IPT-related training appears to have a positive effect on reform attitude and subjective norm and no significant effect on perceived behavioral control; (2) Road Show IV appears to have a positive effect on reform attitude, but no significant effect on subjective norm or perceived behavioral control; and (3) acquisition training appears to have largely insignificant effects on all three factors.

Given that attitude and subjective norm vary to some degree based on IPT training and Road Show IV participation, it will be useful to examine how underlying subfactors differ between those participating in these two training programs and those not participating in these training programs. Based on these results, we analyze how IPT and Road Show IV training affect the outcome beliefs and outcome evaluations that underlie attitudes toward reform. We also analyze how IPT training affects the normative beliefs and motivation to comply that underlie subjective norms toward reform behavior. In this way, it is easier to understand why attitude and subjective norm vary.

Five conclusions can be drawn from the analysis. They are described below.

IPT and Road Show Training Affect Attitude Through Outcome Beliefs

IPT training does affect outcome beliefs. IPT training is related to statistically significantly higher $B \times E$ products on eight outcomes. Differences in outcome beliefs are important to the positive change in each $B \times E$ product. Specifically, those with IPT training are more likely to believe that eliminating milspecs and standards will reduce program costs, improve product quality, reduce program delays, improve ability to meet work objectives, encourage commercial firms to do government work, require learning new skills, increase my responsibilities, and increase cooperation with contractors.

Employees who have participated in IPT training are more likely to believe that these eight—largely positive outcomes of reform—will result.

Of the 23 outcomes surveyed, Road Show IV is related to significantly higher $B \times E$ products on only three: reduce program costs, encourage commercial firms to do government work, and increase cooperation with contractors.

The increase in $B \times E$ product for these three outcomes is related largely to differences in outcome beliefs. Road Show IV attendees are more likely to believe that these outcomes will result from the elimination of milspecs and standards. It appears that the Road Show IV program has been somewhat successful, a major focus of the effort related to the effect of reform on program costs, expanding the industrial base, and improving cooperation with contractors.

IPT Training Affects Subjective Norm Through Normative Beliefs and Motivation to Comply

IPT training affects subjective norm toward reform through both normative beliefs and motivations to comply. Results indicate that IPT training is associated with statistically significant increases in the level of $NB \times MC$ product for all three immediate referents: supervisors, PMs, and co-workers. In each case the increase in $NB \times MC$ product is the result of differences in normative beliefs between those with and without IPT training. Those with IPT training had statistically significantly higher normative beliefs about immediate referents. Those with IPT training are more likely to view their immediate referents as supportive of reform. IPT training also affects the normative beliefs of respondents with respect to the user of the products of the acquisition system.

For the remaining 10 of the 14 referents, differences in motivation to comply are the primary determinant of change in the $NB \times MC$ product. Specifically, IPT training increases the motivation to comply with acquisition leadership (ASA(ALT) and PEO), matrix leadership (commanders of AMC and the buying command), and non-Army referents (Secretary of Defense, OSD staff, industry, Congress, and the public). IPT training appears to have had the desired effect in promoting better communication and understanding between the various players in the acquisition process.

Road Show IV Does Not Affect Subjective Norm or Perceived Behavioral Control

Results of this study also reveal that Road Show IV training is insignificant in the prediction of subjective norm and perceived behavioral control levels. With regard to subjective norm, those who have attended Road Show IV are no more likely than those who have not to view any of the 19 referents surveyed as supportive of (or opposed to) the elimination of milspecs and standards. In addition, those with Road Show IV training are no more likely than those without to believe that eliminating milspecs and standards will be easy, or facilitated by environmental and/or policy factors.

IPT Training Does Not Affect Perceived Behavioral Control

As in Road Show IV training, the study shows that IPT training does not have a significant effect on employees' perceptions of behavioral control. Exposure to IPT training does not appear to provide participants with any greater (or lesser) degree of confidence in the ability of environmental or policy factors to facilitate (or constrain) reform behavior.

Traditional Acquisition Courses Do Not Affect Reform Attitudes, Subjective Norm, or Perceived Behavioral Control

The study shows that traditional acquisition courses conducted through the DAU have no statistically significant effect on employees' attitudes, subjective norms, or perception of behavioral control toward reform behavior. These courses, however, are designed to teach acquisition and procurement management, and are not necessarily designed to facilitate implementation of milspec and standard reform. It is interesting to note, however, that those who have attended these courses are no different from those who have not in terms of their reform attitudes, subjective norm, and perception of behavioral control.

The preceding chapters have analyzed the differences in underlying subfactors to better understand variation in attitude, subjective norm, and perceived behavioral control across career groups, experience level, and organizational affiliation. In addition, we have analyzed the differences in underlying subfactors related to IPT training and Road Show IV attendance, allowing us to assess the effectiveness of these programs and better understand the differences they create in underlying subfactors. Drawing on this information, the final chapter offers specific recommendations on how current efforts to implement milspec and standard elimination can be improved.

Chapter Eleven

IMPROVING IMPLEMENTATION
OF MILSPEC AND STANDARD REFORM

We really don't care about what bureaucrats think, we care what they do.

—James Q. Wilson, *Bureaucracy*

[C]hanges take not only resources, but time, particularly administrative changes which must be reckoned not in months or years but in decades, even generations. What is involved is changing administrative norms, organizational cultures, managerial attitudes, work habits, even social values, and this takes much time, much more time than changing titles, laws, structures, methods, and personnel.

—Gerald E. Caiden,
in R. Baker (ed.), *Comparative Public Management*

Understanding the determinants of bureaucratic behavior in the Army acquisition system is a worthwhile academic goal, but does it have utility in the policy realm? This utility would be realized through the application of our knowledge of bureaucratic behavior to the evaluation and design of implementation policy.

The goal of this study has been to answer three policy questions:

- Is military specification and standard reform being implemented successfully by Army acquisition bureaucrats?

- What factors or determinants affect the willingness and ability of Army acquisition employees to implement milspec and standard reform?

- Having assessed implementation to date and understanding better what affects bureaucratic behavior, how can the Army best affect (align) the underlying beliefs and perceptions (subfactors) of its personnel in order to influence behavior in support of milspec and standard reform?

THE STATE OF IMPLEMENTATION

Do existing implementation efforts need improvement? This is a question that can only be answered by Army leadership. Are they satisfied with the existing level of support for, and implementation of, the policy? The study shows there is a fair degree of support for the policy, and bureaucrats are largely behaving in accordance with the policy. In the sample used here, 66 percent of respondents support reform and 65 percent indicate that they are eliminating milspecs and standards. This could certainly be improved, and the analysis of this study has shown that intentions to implement the policy are, to some degree, countered by negative perceptions of behavioral control: bureaucrats in many instances feel that actually implementing the policy is too difficult.

THE IMPORTANCE OF BEHAVIORAL DETERMINANTS

According to the causal model used here, reform behavior—the elimination of milspecs and standards—is determined by an employee's intention to eliminate milspecs and standards, and his/her perception of behavioral controls. Intention to reform is itself determined by reform attitude and reform subjective norm. Reform behavior is, therefore, ultimately determined by attitude, subjective norm, and perceived behavioral control. Applying the model to the survey data on the Army acquisition work force reveals that attitude, subjective norm, and perceived behavioral control are significantly related to the level of reform intention and reform behavior.

Implications of Strong Bureaucratic Attitudes

Bureaucrats can have positive or negative attitudes toward eliminating milspecs and standards. This attitude depends on the bureaucrat's evaluation of the desirability and likelihood of various outcomes (both personal and programmatic) occurring as a result of the reforms. Estimation of the behavioral model indicates that reform attitude has a strong effect on reform intention, which in turn has a strong effect on reform behavior. The importance of attitude in the prediction of reform intention and behavior implies that policy-makers should pay close attention to the attitudes of their employees. In cases where employee attitude hinders reform behavior, steps might be taken to change attitudes. Such steps might include a communication or persuasion campaign, intensified training, or other direct efforts to change attitudes.

Any communication or training program should focus on the underlying subfactors that determine an employee's attitude toward reform.

Implications of Strong Subjective Norms

Subjective norm represents the effect of social controls, both internal and external, on bureaucratic behavior. Reform implementation strategies should account for the extent to which referent groups are applying pressure and influencing behavior.

Since subjective norm toward reform is significant in the prediction of reform intention and ultimately reform behavior, it is possible for policymakers to leverage referents to further the goals of milspec and standard reform. Specific referents can be identified as important in explaining differences in reform behavior, and they can be included in implementation and training efforts. If beliefs about certain referents are hindering reform behavior, underlying subfactors related to them are subject to change, and this may be an effective strategy for developing or modifying communications and training programs.

Implications of a Strong Perceived Behavioral Control

Perceived behavioral control represents the effect of perceived rules or constraints on one's ability to behave or act in accord with reform. The greater the perception of behavioral control by an acquisition employee, the stronger the behavior (in this case, compliance with the policy to eliminate milspecs and standards).

Perceived behavioral control is determined by the aggregation of control beliefs: beliefs as to whether a given control factor will make it harder or easier to implement milspec and standard reform. The average level of perceived behavioral control in the acquisition work force is negative, indicating which employees on average view the rules they face as making it harder to implement milspec and standard reform. Perceived behavioral control levels, therefore, dampen the generally positive effect of reform intention on reform behavior. The strength of perceived behavioral control's relationship to reform behavior, and the negative perceptions of behavioral control in the work force, imply that the Army should make an effort to change these perceptions—to educate employees on how the control factors will not hinder their ability to reform. A key point is that these are perceived behavioral controls. Policymakers should consider ways to reduce the perception of negative control in the work place. This might be accomplished through a communication and training program.

Implications of Variation in Reform Attitude, Subjective Norm, and Perceived Behavioral Control

Levels of reform attitude, subjective norm, and perceived behavioral control vary throughout the work force. For example, military personnel hold much higher attitude, subjective norm, and perceived behavioral control levels compared to engineering, QA, and logistics personnel. Differences such as this imply that implementation behavior will also vary across these groups.

RECOMMENDATIONS FOR CHANGING REFORM BEHAVIOR

The observations and recommendations provided in this chapter assume that the differences in attitude, subjective norm, and perceived behavioral control found in the work force are worth addressing and aligning. This study assumes that the goal of current reform implementation and training initiatives is to "convert" as many employees as possible to the goal of eliminating milspecs and standards from use in Army acquisition.

To change reform behavior, policymakers might try to change the factors that affect it: attitude, subjective norm, perceived behavioral control, and their subfactors.

Based on the analysis of this study, two overarching recommendations are made for the Army leadership:

- Use and improve existing training programs—IPT and Road Show IV training—to change reform attitude, subjective norm, and perceived behavioral control; and

- Target implementation efforts to the resistant elements of the work force, focusing on the alignment underlying subfactors between those employees who are resisting reform and those meeting implementation objectives.

Use and Improve Existing Training Programs

This study examined the effects of three training programs—traditional acquisition management courses, IPT training, and Road Show IV training—on reform attitude, subjective norm, and perceived behavioral control. Two of the training programs—IPT training and Road Show IV training—were found to be related to the determinants of reform behavior. Specifically, IPT training is related to significantly higher values on reform attitude and subjective norm. Road Show IV training is related to significantly higher reform attitude. None of the training programs studied had a significant effect on perceived behavioral control.

The positive and significant effects of IPT and Road Show IV training programs on reform attitude and subjective norm suggest that these programs should continue to be used to implement milspec and standard reform. The fact that neither training program (especially Road Show IV) has any effect on perceived behavioral control is disappointing. If the Army wishes to promote milspec and standard reform, efforts must be taken to educate employees that many of the barriers to reform behavior they perceive do not exist—such as the belief that acquisition laws do not support the elimination of milspecs and standards.

Expand IPT training. IPT training has a significant effect on the level of reform attitude and subjective norm. More important to the objective of aligning underlying subfactors, IPT training is significantly related to the level of several outcome beliefs and to the level of normative beliefs and motivations to comply with a number of referent groups. Basically, IPT training is associated with changes in underlying subfactors that bring beliefs into greater alignment. For example, IPT-trained respondents are more likely to believe that milspec and standard reform will result in improvements in quality.

As noted above, IPT training is positively statistically significantly related to higher reform attitude and subjective norm values. This implies greater reform intention and behavior. Given these positive and significant effects, it is advisable to continue IPT training efforts. Given the positive effects of IPT training on milspec and standard reform, and the Army's goal of using more IPTs in the acquisition process, it is advisable to expand the program to reach more Army acquisition employees.

The fact that the primary objective of IPT training is to facilitate IPT implementation is quite important to the recommendations made here. IPT training's positive effect on the level of attitude and subjective norm related to the elimination of milspecs and standards is simply a by-product of the training, not its primary objective. Recognizing that this is neither a primary goal nor a justification, these recommendations call for the continued use of IPT training in order to gain the by-product benefits for milspec and standard reform. Therefore, we make no specific recommendations calling for the alteration or improvement of IPT training to further milspec and standard reform directly.

One difficulty with this recommendation is that there is not a single, standardized form of IPT training in the Army or the DoD. For the purposes of this study, IPT training is measured as participation in at least one of four IPT training programs. These training programs are: (1) formal DoD training, (2) external training, (3) prime/subcontractor provided training, and (4) internal Army training. This analysis concludes only that participation in one or more of these types of IPT training is significantly related to the level of reform attitude, subjective norm, and their underlying subfactors.

Expand and improve Road Show training. Road Show IV was specifically designed to further the objectives of milspec and standard reform, having as a major focus training on how to replace milspecs and standards with performance specs. Analysis indicates that participation in Road Show IV is related to statistically significantly higher reform attitude, reform intention, and reform behavior. Table 10.1 showed that Road Show IV attendance ranged from 19 to 31 percent across the five career groups surveyed for this study. Given its success, Road Show type training—focusing specifically on milspec and standard reform—should be provided to a greater number of Army acquisition employees.

There is evidence that Road Show training can be even more effective if improved. While designed to persuade, educate, and train employees on the desirability and utility of milspec and standard reform, Road Show IV failed to have any significant impact on reform subjective norm and perceived behavioral control: two important determinants of reform intention and reform behavior. Given the stated purpose of Road Show training—taking the reform message on the road, communicating leadership goals and the appropriate methods to meet them—the lack of a relationship between the training program and the level of reform subjective norm, perceived behavioral control, is disappointing. If redesigned to target resistant elements and specifically the subfactors underlying subjective norm and perceived behavioral control, Road Show training could be even more effective and useful in implementing milspec and standard reform.

If we are to truly improve implementation of milspec reform, IPT and Road Show training must be improved to help align the specific underlying subfactors of acquisition employees identified in Chapters Seven, Eight, and Nine.

Target Resistant Elements and Align Underlying Subfactors

Perhaps this study's greatest utility lies in the information generated on how the underlying subfactors of respondents vary across career group, experience level, and organization. The comparison of underlying subfactors helps to explain why various groups differ in their reform attitude, subjective norm, and perceived behavioral control. The basis of this recommendation and the subrecommendations described below is that aligning the underlying subfactors of those with lower attitude, subjective norm, and perceived behavioral control values with those who have higher values will result in greater compliance with the directive to eliminate milspecs and standards.

Chapters Seven, Eight, and Nine identified a number of important underlying subfactors that differentiate those who do and do not support implementation of milspec and standard reform. One strategy to improve implementation of milspec and standard reform would be to increase the levels of the subfactors of the "do not" groups to the level of the "do" groups. This alignment may be possible by targeting resistant elements, using and improving existing training programs, and taking advantage of information gained in this study to improve future implementation efforts.

The subrecommendations below identify objectives for policymakers that can be incorporated into implementation programs and planning. They recommend new areas of focus for an implementation effort based on the analysis and information provided in this study. Since there is only a fixed quantity of funds available for training and implementation efforts, these recommendations suggest that such efforts should focus on the more resistant career groups (engineers, QAs, and logisticians), matrix employees, and experienced employees. In this manner, training and implementation funds can be directed to where they will have the greatest impact. Underlying the recommendations suggesting targeting of resistant elements is the old adage "Don't preach to the choir."

Target QA, engineering, and logistics personnel. A central aspect of this study has been to locate the significant differences in reform attitude, subjective norm, and perceived behavioral control within the Army acquisition work force. Military and contracting personnel hold the highest attitude, subjective norm, and perceived behavioral control values. These higher values translate into higher reform intentions and greater compliance with the policy to eliminate milspecs and standards. Statistically significantly lower attitude, subjective norm, and perceived behavioral control values are held by engineering, QA, and logistics personnel. By far the lowest values are held by QA personnel. These lower values translate into lower reform intentions and less compliance with the policy to eliminate mil-specs and standards.

Targeting training and implementation efforts on resistant elements should focus primarily on QA personnel. QA personnel hold the lowest reform attitude, subjective norm, and perceived behavioral control values by far. In fact, QA personnel are the only group to actually hold a negative reform attitude, indicating they do not support the elimination of milspecs and standards. It will also be important to focus efforts on engineering personnel. Engineers are the largest single career group in the acquisition work force. They are involved in all facets of acquisition, from development to sustainment. In addition, the skills of engineers are very important in the development and application of the performance specifications that are replacing traditional milspecs and standards. Support for and adherence to the policy by engineers may well be very important to the policy's success.

Target matrix employees. Even though QA, engineering, and logistics personnel are mostly affiliated with matrix organizations, this analysis shows that matrix personnel have significantly lower reform attitude and subjective norm than PM personnel do. Reform of the milspecs and standards system may also be served by focusing a portion of implementation and training efforts on matrix personnel generally.

Such a targeted program might focus training and implementation efforts on major subordinate and buying commands (the home of matrix organizations). These efforts would take training and implementation efforts into the functional divisions resident within these commands: engineering, QA, logistics, and contracting.

Target experienced employees. The analysis further indicates that employees who have been involved in acquisition for more than 20 years hold a significantly lower reform attitude than do employees with under 20 years experience. Training and implementation efforts can be targeted to this group as well. Specifically, training efforts can be directed at addressing the concerns of this group.

Changing the reform-related attitude, subjective norm and perceived behavioral control of resistant employees will require efforts to better align their underlying subfactors with those of the more supportive employees. The following recommendations are designed to move underlying subfactors into better alignment.

Address outcome beliefs to change attitude. This study has shown a set of 10 outcome beliefs to be key to understanding differences in attitude toward reform between the three civilian career groups (engineering, QA, and logistics) and military personnel. To better align outcome beliefs and thus attitudes between the more resistant civilian groups and the military, Army leaders should (1) better educate engineers, QAs, and logisticians that seven potentially positive outcomes of reform are possible, and (2) better educate the same group that three potentially negative outcomes are unlikely to result from eliminating milspecs and standards. Specifically, training and communication programs need to convince resistant elements that the following positive outcomes will be realized, or are likely to be realized, as a result of reform: improve product quality; improve ability to meet work objectives; increase cooperation with contractors; increase responsibilities; encourage commercial firms to do government work; make program management easier; and reduce program delays.

In addition, these efforts should focus on limiting and reversing fears within the engineering, QA, and logistics communities that the following negative outcomes are unlikely to result from the elimination of milspecs and standards: increase life cycle costs; reduce my authority; and reduce competition in the spares market.

To the extent that outcome beliefs related to these outcomes can be addressed and changed, the alignment of underlying outcome beliefs will be improved.

Eight of the 10 outcome beliefs discussed above relate to programmatic outcomes, rather than personal outcomes. One important conclusion is that differences in beliefs between the various groups (career group, experience level, organization) were most often related to differences in beliefs (outcome evaluations or outcome beliefs) related to programmatic rather than personal outcomes. Programmatic outcomes refer to outcomes related to a given acquisition program; they are commonly thought of as cost, schedule, and performance outcomes. On the other hand, personal outcomes relate to outcomes that affect a bureaucrat personally, such as workload, authority, responsibility, and remuneration.

Results have shown that across groups there were no real differences in beliefs related to personal outcomes. Therefore, any modifications to existing training and implementation efforts are likely to be best served by emphasizing how milspec and standard reform can benefit programmatic outcomes. In addition, this finding implies that Army leadership need not focus a great deal of attention on how to incentivize reform behavior with personal rewards and benefits. This recommendation is not meant to imply that all personal outcomes and effects should be ignored in devising new implementation and training programs: programmatic outcomes should be given priority.

While the formulation of specific programs to address these outcome beliefs is a job for Army leaders and trainers, it should be possible to specifically address these outcomes and issues. Understanding that many employees are concerned that an outcome—such as improvement in quality—is relatively unlikely to result from eliminating milspecs and standards, time should be devoted to changing this belief. Such an effort might include presentation of analysis supporting the likelihood of an outcome, or it could include presentations of lessons learned or examples where an outcome was actually realized as a result of reform. Such lessons learned or examples of success are more likely to be available as time goes by. Given that the elimination of milspecs and standards has been going on for over two years, such examples may soon be available.

Address normative beliefs to change subjective norm. This study has shown that differences in normative beliefs, or the combination of differences in normative beliefs and motivation to comply, determine the majority of the changes in $NB \times MC$ product (and thus changes in subjective norm) when the underlying subfactors of the civilian career groups and military personnel are compared. Specifically, it was determined that engineers, QAs, and logisticians (1) hold lower normative beliefs with regard to immediate referents, (2) hold lower normative beliefs and motivations to comply with Army acquisition leadership, and (3) are more motivated to comply with matrix leadership. Aligning the normative beliefs and motivation to comply for these referent groups should be an objective of any improved training and communication programs.

To help align normative beliefs, new training and communication efforts must continue to emphasize the role and support of immediate referents in the elimination of milspecs and standards. In particular, steps must be taken to convince employees that their co-workers support the reform effort. This will be difficult. One suggestion is to apply training programs to office or organizational groups, so that co-workers can share the same training experience. Another might be to conduct follow-up or focus group–type sessions with groups of co-workers to allow open discussion of milspec and standard reform. Such sessions would take place with facilitators who are trained to address employee concerns about the reform and also have the ability to correct and address misperceptions about the intent and potential effects of reform. At a minimum, training efforts must include supervisors and PMs. In addition, normative beliefs about these actors can be bolstered by using them in follow-up sessions with their employees where milspec and standard reform are discussed and training is continued. Any effort to demonstrate the commitment, participation, and support of supervisors and PMs will help to bolster normative beliefs within the work force.

Designing new training and communication programs to better align normative beliefs related to acquisition leadership might improve subjective norms toward reform behavior. To accomplish this, training programs must do even more to emphasize the support of ASA(ALT) and the PEOs for reform. Toward this end, even greater participation of ASA(ALT), representatives of ASA(ALT), and the PEOs in training and communication efforts would be advisable. Another option would be to allow direct PEO involvement in all efforts directed at the programs and personnel under its supervision. While acquisition leadership has already been greatly involved in the Road Show process, it is disappointing that engineers, QAs, logisticians, and matrix personnel believe them to be relatively less supportive of the reform effort. Any steps taken to emphasize to these groups the commitment of ASA(ALT) and the PEOs to the elimination of milspecs and standards will better align the beliefs important in explaining variation in subjective norm.

Since matrix employees and QA personnel hold a significantly lower subjective norm toward reform, it may well be possible to increase their subjective norm toward reform by leveraging their motivation to comply with matrix leadership. While this recommendation does not serve to better align motivation, it does recommend taking advantage of existing motivations to bring resistant groups into greater compliance. If these groups are convinced that matrix leadership supports the reform effort and is committed to it (normative belief), they may be much more positively disposed toward the elimination of milspecs and standards. Therefore, it is recommended that future training and communication efforts involve to the greatest extent possible members of matrix leadership and management. Efforts must be taken to convince employees that the commander of AMC, AMC managers, other matrix managers, and the commanders of the buying command support the reform.

Address control beliefs to change perceptions of behavioral control. Engineers, QAs, and logisticians have significantly different control beliefs compared to military personnel. To better align control beliefs, efforts should be made to directly address control factors and control issues in an attempt to modify employee perceptions. In addition, to the extent possible, steps should be taken to minimize the real constraining effects (if any) of the surveyed control factors. There are three types of control factors surveyed in this study: (1) policy factors, (2) rule factors, and (3) environmental factors. Recommendations for each are provided below.

Policy factors are control factors that describe policies and elements put in place to facilitate milspec and standard reform. These include the training provided, information on how to eliminate milspecs and standards, the discretion provided, and information on how to work without milspecs and standards. In general, the three civilian career groups find these factors to be inadequate, or less effective in facilitating reform behavior of civilians than of military personnel. Future training and communication efforts need to place much greater attention on teaching participants how to eliminate milspecs and standards and how to work, or perform their job, without milspecs and standards. The Road Show IV program provided case study training on how to write and implement a performance specification rather than a milspec. Perhaps future efforts should take this exam-

ple further and provide added cases and/or more exposure to the issues involved in eliminating milspecs and doing one's job without
them. In addition, case studies are by necessity general. If future
programs are less centralized and tailored more to individual programs and functions, specific case studies can be devised that are
more salient or relevant to participants; this may improve understanding of how to eliminate and work without milspecs and standards.

Almost across the board, civilian personnel perceive acquisition
laws, Army acquisition regulations, and standard operating procedures to be relatively more constraining on their ability to eliminate
milspecs and standards than do military personnel. In this instance,
training and communication efforts need to emphasize educating
employees on recent changes to acquisition laws and regulations. It
is important to deliver the message that current laws and regulations
do not preclude the elimination of milspecs and standards. In some
instances, particular career groups or functions may have particular
concerns relating to specific laws and regulations; trainers and facilitators may be able to address these concerns. Control beliefs related
to laws and regulations may also be addressed through means other
than direct training. Targeted communication efforts (memos and
other publications) can be directed to employees who address these
issues and even specific concerns of different groups.

External or environmental constraints—availability of funds, time,
human resources, and skilled employees—are the most difficult to
deal with, due to the influence of external actors such as DoD oversight activities and the appropriators in Congress. Where the effect
of environmental constraints is perceptual, effort should be undertaken to change perception. In most cases, however, perceptions of
environmental constraints are based on the reality of experience. To
the degree possible, efforts should be made to lessen these constraints, hopefully changing perceptions along the way. One control
factor—the skills of others—is probably the most easily addressed by
Army management. In this case, improved training may affect the
skill base enough to change perceptions. However, to the extent that
perceptions of the skills of others are based on basic management
and/or technical skills, control beliefs can only be corrected over
time through appropriate human resource policies. The remaining
factors relate to the availability of funds, time, and human resources.

To a degree, these constraints are real and are an aspect of the post–Cold War environment. They may not be correctable.

SUMMARY RECOMMENDATION: USE AN IMPROVED ROAD SHOW TRAINING PROGRAM

To summarize, the recommendations above call upon Army leadership to intensify their implementation and training efforts with respect to milspec and standard reform. Using the information generated in this study, these recommendations advise Army leaders to "avoid preaching to the choir." Focus implementation efforts on the elements of the work force exhibiting the greatest resistance to reform. In large part, this effort can be conducted through existing training programs. IPT training has proved quite effective in changing reform attitude and subjective norm. Road Show training has been effective in changing reform attitude. To be most effective, implementation and training efforts need to focus on not only the resistant elements of the work force but also the underlying subfactors that characterize their individual resistance. Perhaps, underlying subfactors can best be addressed through an improved and expanded Road Show training program. Such a program would build upon the suggestions above to improve the Road Show effect on normative beliefs and extend it to the subfactors important in determining subjective norm and perceived behavioral control.

Although not stated explicitly in the analysis above, perhaps the best way to expand Road Show training, address resistant elements, and change their beliefs is through a decentralized and tailored Road Show program. While Road Show IV was conducted at major subordinate and buying commands, its focus was general and its attendance was limited. Given the fact that reform attitude, subjective norm, and perceived behavioral control vary largely by career group, experience level, and organization, it might be worthwhile to decentralize the Road Show program and tailor it to specific functional groups (engineering, QA, logistics) and/or programs (specific PEO programs or PM offices). In this manner, training programs can be tailored to local conditions and emphasis can be placed on immediate referents. In addition, such a tailored program can provide training specific to local concerns and programs, providing more relevance to the training process. This process should be viewed as continual activity. Road Show training needs to be repeated, and there needs to be follow-up by relevant PMs and supervisors. A decentralized training program—modeled on Road Show—that incorporates the recommendations made above, coupled with an ongoing and expanded IPT training program, holds great promise for increasing reform attitude, subjective norm, and perceived behavioral control, thus influencing positively the adoption of the milspecs and standards policy by the acquisition work force.

Finally, it is important to point out that these recommendations assume that the goal of Army leadership is the widespread adoption of milspec and standard reform by all employees. It may well be the case that Army leadership has determined that only specific groups need support the reform. If this is the case, the targets of training and implementation efforts may well be different groups. If, for example, Army leaders have determined that QA personnel are not essential to the successful application of this policy, they will not be targeted. However, the information provided in this study will assist in any targeting effort. This study has determined the relative levels of attitude, subjective norm, perceived behavioral control, reform intention, and reform behavior within the acquisition work force. Army leaders now have relative benchmarks upon which to judge the penetration of the policy into different career groups. Based on the overall reform strategy and goals of Army leadership, different targeting schemes may be appropriate. If, however, the goal is acceptance of the policy across the work force, it may pay to target training and implementation efforts on QA, engineering, and logistics personnel in order to better align their underlying subfactors or beliefs.

In the end, the utility and relevance of this research lies in the value of the information provided to policymakers. The purpose of this study is to identify relationships and beliefs within the work force that when changed hold the promise of improving implementation of milspec and standard reform. Suggesting how the Army might adapt its current implementation efforts to better align the underlying subfactors that contribute to reform attitude, subjective norm, and perceived behavioral control should help policymakers think about implementation strategies. Going beyond suggestion and actually determining how best to redesign and implement programs is really the job of Army policymakers. How they tackle this challenge will be based on many factors in addition to the information on bureaucratic behavior provided in this study.

ANALYTIC METHODS

As outlined in Chapter Five, we conducted a comprehensive survey of Army acquisition personnel to provide a measurement of the various factors in the theory of planned behavior model. The survey was administered to a stratified random sample of 3,000 Army acquisition employees; 1,774 responses were received (59 percent response rate). After "cleaning" the data by removing incomplete observations and those with indicator variable values in excess of three standard deviations from the mean, the analyzed sample had 1,653 observations.

SEM/LVM ANALYSIS

To apply the theory of planned behavior to the data from the survey, we employed a form of causal modeling known as Structural Equations Modeling (SEM)/Latent Variable Modeling (LVM). This method is characterized by Barbara Byrne:

> The term structural equation modeling conveys two important aspects of the procedure: (a) that the causal processes under study are represented by a series of structural (i.e., regression) equations, and (b) that these structural relations can be modeled pictorially to enable a clearer conceptualization of the theory under study. The hypothesized model can then be tested statistically in a simultaneous analysis of the entire system of variables to determine the extent to which it is consistent with the data. If goodness of fit is adequate, the model argues for the plausibility of postulated relations among variables; if it is inadequate, the tenability of such relations is rejected (Byrne, 1994, p. 3).

Latent variables are unobservable. An example frequently used for a latent variable is intelligence. There are a variety of IQ tests, and these tests result in differing indicators of the latent variable: intelligence. In SEM/LVM, multiple indicators of latent variables are used. Using multiple indicators has a distinct advantage over approaches that use a single indicator to represent each latent variable (such as path analysis). For example, the result of one IQ test is an indicator of intelligence. Using a single indicator requires the assumption that a variable has been measured perfectly (i.e., without error). Multiple indicators allow more reliability by identifying and taking into account measurement error (Bentler, 1995; Bentler and Wu, 1995; Byrne, 1994; Pedhazur, 1982; Reinecke, Schmidt, and Ajzen, 1996).

There are, therefore, two models in SEM/LVM analysis: (1) the measurement model, which represents the relationship between indicator variables and the latent variables composing the model; and (2) the structural model, which represents the relations among the model's latent variables (Bentler, 1995; Bentler and Wu, 1995; Byrne, 1994). Figure A.1 shows the structural model. In it, attitude, subjective norm, perceived behavioral control, reform intention, and reform behavior are the latent variables. As with intelligence, these variables are unobservable, although there are various indicators of them. Any single indicator is related to a latent variable with error, and the use of multiple indicators allows this error to be identified and accounted for in model estimation. This is accomplished in the measurement model.

A measurement model represents the relationship between the model's latent variables and some set of indicator variables. Specifically, the measurement model postulates that the indicator variables are equal to some linear function of the latent variables plus an error term. This implies that the latent variable is a common factor explaining the covariation among the indicator variables. The strength of the relationship between the indicator variables and the latent factor is measured by "factor loadings"—interpreted similarly to regression coefficients (Bentler, 1995; Byrne, 1994). The higher a given indicator variable's factor loading, the better the internal consistency of the latent variable, and the better it is in explaining variation in the latent variable (Reinecke, Schmidt, and Ajzen, 1996).

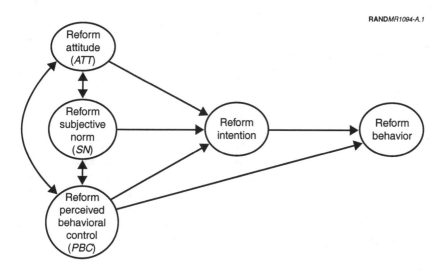

Figure A.1—Structural Model of Planned Behavior

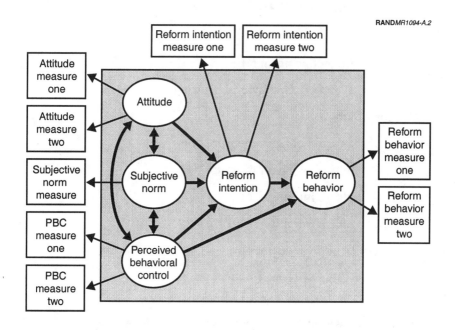

Figure A.2—SEM/LVM Structural and Measurement Model

A SEM/LVM model is a combined structural and measurement model (Bentler, 1995; Bentler and Wu, 1995; Byrne, 1994). The complete SEM/LVM (measurement and structural model) employed in this analysis is presented in Figure A.2. The latent variables in the structural model are shown by circles.[1] Indicator variables used for the latent variables in the measurement model are shown by rectangles.

The structural model is enclosed in the box at the center of Figure A.2. Indicator variables used in the measurement model lie outside the box. The arrows from the various latent variables outside the box to each separate indicator variable are "factor loadings" showing which indicators are associated with which latent variables. This latent variable model—both structural and measurement—can be summarized by the following relationships:

Latent variables or factors:

   RB: Reform behavior (1)

   RI: Reform intention (2)

   ATT: Attitude (3)

   SN: Subjective norm (4)

   PBC: Perceived behavioral control (5)

Indicator variables:

   *B*1: Reform behavior measure one

   *B*2: Reform behavior measure two

   *I*1: Reform intention measure one

   *I*2: Reform intention measure two

   *A*1: Attitude measure one

   *A*2: Attitude measure two

---

[1]Subjective norm is identified as a latent variable. Unlike the other latent variables, it is measured with only one indicator variable and not with multiple indicators.

S: Subjective norm measure

*P*1: Perceived behavioral control measure one

*P*2: Perceived behavioral control measure two

Structural model (standardized coefficients)

$$RB = b_{12}RI + b_{15}PBC + e$$
$$RI = b_{23}ATT + b_{24}SN + b_{25}PBC + e$$

Measurement model (standardized coefficients):

$$B1 = b_{B11}RB + e$$
$$B2 = b_{B21}RB + e$$
$$I1 = b_{I12}RI + e$$
$$I2 = b_{I22}RI + e$$
$$A1 = b_{A13}ATT + e$$
$$A2 = b_{A23}ATT + e$$
$$S = b_{S4}SN + e$$
$$P1 = b_{P15}PBC + e$$
$$P2 = b_{P25}PBC + e$$

The structural model of reform behavior (Figure A.1) shows relations between attitude, subjective norm, perceived behavioral control, reform intention, and reform behavior. The measurement model identifies indicator variables associated with each of these latent variables. These models were estimated and tested using "EQS for Macintosh" (Bentler, 1995; Bentler and Wu, 1995; Byrne, 1994), a structural equation modeling software package.

THE MEASUREMENT MODEL

In this study all latent variables in the model are represented by multiple indicators except for subjective norm. The indicator variables are global measures of attitude, subjective norm, perceived behavioral control, reform intention, and reform behavior. Each global measure or indicator variable is one survey item designed to measure the latent variable. Table A.1 shows the survey items used to measure each of the indicator variables. Each of the items was presented in the survey as follows:

- **Attitude measure one (A1).** "I support the elimination of milspecs and standards (from use in current Army RFPs, SOWs, contracts and other acquisition activities)."[2] Respondents were asked the degree to which they supported this statement, from strong agreement to strong disagreement.

- **Attitude measure two (A2).** "Eliminating the military specifications you use in your job (from use in current Army RFPs, SOWs, contracts and other acquisition activities) is . . . ?" Respondents were asked to indicate the degree of desirability, from very desirable to very undesirable.

- **Subjective norm (S).** "Considering the people whose opinions are important in the decisions you make on the job, how likely or unlikely is it that they support the elimination of milspecs and standards (from use in current Army RFPs, SOWs, contracts and other acquisition activities) in your job?" Respondents were asked to indicate the degree of likely support, from very likely to very unlikely.

- **Perceived behavioral control measure one (P1).** "Thinking about what it will take to implement the policy (to eliminate milspecs and standards from use in current Army RFPs, SOWs, contracts and other acquisition activities), how difficult will it be for you to eliminate milspecs and standards from your work?" Respondents were asked to indicate the degree of difficulty, from very easy to very hard.

- **Perceived behavioral control measure two (P2).** "Thinking about working without milspecs and standards, how difficult will it be for you to do your job in an environment without milspecs and standards?" Respondents were asked to indicate the degree of difficulty, from very easy to very hard.

---

[2]The portion in parentheses was included in instructions to the survey section to provide context and time.

Table A.1

Indicator Variables Used in Measurement Model

Variable	Observations	Mean	Standard Deviation	Minimum	Maximum
A1	1,653	0.511	1.823	−3	3
A2	1,653	0.788	1.642	−3	3
S	1,653	1.060	1.500	−3	3
P1	1,653	−0.068	1.805	−3	3
P2	1,653	−0.061	1.726	−3	3
I1	1,653	1.926	0.832	−3	3
I2	1,653	2.118	0.842	−3	3
B1	1,653	0.433	1.665	−3	3
B2	1,653	1.377	1.620	−3	3

- **Reform intention measure one ($I1$).** "I intend to comply, or continue to comply, with directives to eliminate milspecs and standards (from use in current Army RFPs, SOWs, contracts and other acquisition activities)." Respondents were asked the degree to which they supported this statement, from strong agreement to strong disagreement.

- **Reform intention measure two ($I2$).** "If the Army directs me to eliminate milspecs and standards (from use in current Army RFPs, SOWs, contracts and other acquisition activities), it is my responsibility to do so." Respondents were asked the degree to which they supported this statement, from strong agreement to strong disagreement.

- **Reform behavior measure one ($B1$).** "I no longer use milspecs and standards (in current Army RFPs, SOWs, contracts and other acquisition activities) in my job." Respondents were asked the degree to which they supported this statement, from strong agreement to strong disagreement.

- **Reform behavior measure two ($B2$).** "How likely is it that you do not use or cite any milspecs or standards in the RFP or SOW?" Respondents were asked to indicate the likelihood that they pursue this course of action, from very likely to very unlikely.

The correlation and covariance matrices for the indicator variables are provided in Tables A.2 and A.3.

Table A.2

Correlation Matrix

	A1	A2	S	P1	P2	I1	I2
A1	1						
A2	0.728	1					
S	0.455	0.472	1				
P1	0.360	0.374	0.237	1			
P2	0.509	0.528	0.335	0.631	1		
I1	0.307	0.319	0.265	0.149	0.211	1	
I2	0.211	0.219	0.182	0.102	0.145	0.493	1
B1	0.226	0.234	0.170	0.198	0.280	0.301	0.207
B2	0.170	0.177	0.129	0.150	0.211	0.227	0.156
ATT	0.838	0.869	0.543	0.430	0.608	0.367	0.252
PBC	0.539	0.559	0.355	0.668	0.945	0.223	0.153
RI	0.363	0.377	0.313	0.176	0.249	0.847	0.582
RB	0.342	0.355	0.259	0.300	0.425	0.456	0.314

	B1	B2	ATT	PBC	RI	RB
A1						
A2						
S						
P1						
P2						
I1						
I2						
B1	1					
B2	0.328	1				
ATT	0.269	0.203	1			
PBC	0.296	0.224	0.643	1		
RI	0.355	0.268	0.433	0.264	1	
RB	0.659	0.498	0.408	0.450	0.539	1

In Table A.1, higher means indicate a more favorable response for the variables in question. For example, higher means indicate a more favorable attitude, subjective norm, or perceived behavioral control in relation to eliminating milspecs and standards. Higher values for reform intention variables indicate stronger intent to eliminate milspecs and standards. Finally, higher values on the reform behavior indicators indicate higher perceived levels of compliance with the reform. Based on these mean values, respondents have favorable attitudes and subjective norms. Perceived behavioral

Table A.3

Covariance Matrix

	A1	A2	S	P1	P2	I1	I2
A1	3.322						
A2	2.179	2.695					
S	1.244	1.163	2.249				
P1	1.184	1.107	0.641	3.258			
P2	1.601	1.497	0.867	1.966	2.979		
I1	0.466	0.436	0.331	0.224	0.303	0.692	
I2	0.324	0.303	0.230	0.156	0.210	0.345	0.709
B1	0.684	0.640	0.425	0.595	0.804	0.417	0.290
B2	0.503	0.470	0.313	0.437	0.591	0.306	0.213
ATT	1.527	1.427	0.815	0.776	1.049	0.305	0.212
PBC	0.982	0.918	0.532	1.206	1.630	0.186	0.129
RI	0.466	0.436	0.331	0.224	0.303	0.497	0.345
RB	0.684	0.640	0.425	0.595	0.804	0.417	0.290

	B1	B2	ATT	PBC	RI	RB
A1						
A2						
S						
P1						
P2						
I1						
I2						
B1	2.772					
B2	0.885	2.624				
ATT	0.448	0.329	1			
PBC	0.493	0.363	0.643	1		
RI	0.417	0.306	0.305	0.186	0.497	
RB	1.204	0.885	0.448	0.493	0.417	1.204

control measures, however, are slightly negative, indicating that respondents view perceived behavioral control as contrary to reform. Both reform intention and behavior are positive, with intention stronger than behavior.[3]

---

[3]It is useful to note the large difference in mean values for the reform behavior indicators. SEM/LVM allows for the joint variation in these variables to be used in the analysis of the latent variables affecting reform behavior. Using traditional path analysis, one or the other of these indicators would be used to measure behavior, and very different results might be expected.

As presented in Table A.4, the factor loadings on the indicator variables are relatively high, ranging from 0.50 to 0.95, and all statistically significant at the 1 percent level. This implies that the indicator variables have good internal consistency in approximating the latent variables of the model. Overall, the results indicate the latent variables are measured well.

Table A.4

Factor Loadings for
Model Indicator Variables

Measurement Variable	Factor Loading
A1	.84*
A2	.87*
P1	.67*
P2	.95*
I1	.85*
I2	.58*
B1	.66*
B2	.50*

*p > .01.

THE STRUCTURAL MODEL

Table A.5 shows that the structural model fits the data from the Army acquisition work force well. The goodness of fit is indicated by a robust comparative fit index (RCFI) of 0.948 (reported in Table A.5).[4] As Byrne (1994) notes, good fit suggests "the plausibility of postulated relations among variables." In this context, "good fit" means an RCFI of 0.90 or more. The path coefficients in the standardized solution are shown in Figure A.3 (large unidirectional arrows) and reported in Table A.5 (along with the unstandardized coefficients). All of the hypothesized pathways in the model are statistically signifi-

[4]Reported RCFI values in excess of 0.90 are considered acceptable (Byrne, 1994). Another measure of "fit" is the comparative fit index (CFI). The RCFI was selected since it adjusts for nonnormal data and large sample size. The computed CFI had a value of 0.948 as well, indicating a good fit using this measure.

RAND*MR1094-A.3*

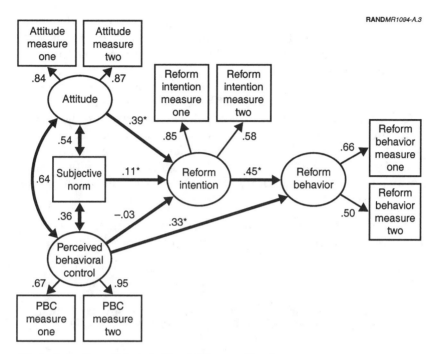

* Indicates path coefficient significant at 1 percent level.

Figure A.3—Predicting Reform Intention and Reform Behavior and
Standardized Coefficients in Theory of Planned Behavior

cant at the 1 percent level, except for the pathway from perceived
behavioral control to reform intention, which is statistically insignificant at the 5 percent level. In addition, Figure A.3 shows the estimated factor loadings between the latent variables and the indicator
variables (small unidirectional arrows) which are all at least 0.50, indicating their usefulness in approximating the latent variables. Finally, the correlation coefficients for the model's exogenous variables
(attitude, subjective norm, and perceived behavioral control) are
shown (large bidirectional arrows).

The first part of the structural model is the prediction of reform intention. As shown in Table A.5, attitude, subjective norm, and perceived behavioral control account for 20 percent of the variance in
reform intention (identified as Stage One in Table A.5). Attitude and

subjective norm are significant predictors of reform intention. Attitude is the most important factor in predicting reform intention, with a standardized coefficient (0.39). This coefficient is more than three times larger than the coefficient on subjective norm (0.11). Both factors have a positive influence on reform intention. Perceived behavioral control is not a statistically significant predictor of reform intention, but does have a direct positive effect on reform behavior. Combined, reform intention and perceived behavioral control account for 39 percent of the variation in reform behavior (identified as Stage Two in Table A.5). Both factors are statistically significant and positive in the prediction of reform behavior, with reform intention having the largest effect.

In sum, the TPB model of bureaucratic behavior fits the data well. The theory accounts for a sizable amount of variance in both the in-

Table A.5

Standardized and Unstandardized Path Coefficients for Structural Model of Reform Behavior, with Goodness of Fit Indices for Model

	Attitude	Subjective Norm	Perceived Behavioral Control	Reform Intention	Percent of Variance Explained
Stage one (reform intention)					
Standardized coefficient (b)	0.391*	0.110*	−0.027	NA	0.20
Regression coefficient (β)	0.276*	0.052*	−0.019	NA	
Stage two (reform behavior)					
Standardized coefficient (b)	NA	NA	0.331*	0.452*	0.39
Regression coefficient (β)	NA	NA	0.363*	0.704*	
Model fit					
Comparative fit index	0.948				
Robust CFI[a]	0.948				

*p > .01.

[a]Robust comparative fit index, adjusting for nonnormal data and large sample size.

tention to discontinue using milspecs and standards (reform intention) and the actual elimination of milspecs and standards (reform behavior). Reform intention depends on Army personnel's attitude toward the reform (good or bad) and their subjective norm in relation to the reforms (perceived support of important work-related referents). The higher the value of reform attitude or subjective norm, the higher is reform intention. Reform behavior is affected by reform intentions and *PBC*. The greater the intention to reform, the higher the level of reform behavior. In addition, the greater the perception of behavioral control within the acquisition work force, the greater the compliance with milspec and standard elimination.

A NOTE ON THE TESTING OF ALTERNATIVE MODELS

Alternative models, using the same variables, were tested to determine their ability to fit the acquisition survey data. While some alternative model forms were found to have a slightly better fit with the data, these models suffered a loss in explained variation in either reform intention or reform behavior. For example, testing a model without the hypothesized pathway between *PBC* and reform intention resulted in a model with a CFI of 0.948, which explained 19.4 percent of the variance in reform intention and 39.5 percent of the variation in reform behavior. Eliminating the insignificant pathway resulted in very little change in model fit and only slight change in its ability to predict intentions and behavior. In another case, estimating the correlation between error terms on selected indicator variables (in this case, reform intention measure two and reform behavior measure two) resulted in a slightly better fit, with a CFI of 0.959, but a drop in the explained variation in reform intention (18.6 percent) and in reform behavior (35 percent). In addition, models with correlated errors are much more complicated to interpret, thus failing to add any parsimony. Finally, alternative model forms were tested that (1) hypothesized direct paths from *ATT* and *SN* to reform behavior, and (2) combined *ATT* and *SN* into a single latent variable. All such models were found to have inadequate fit.

ANALYZING THE EFFECT OF EXTERNAL VARIABLES

In the TPB, variables such as demographic variables, attitudes not directly related to reform behavior,[5] and past behaviors or experiences affect intentions only through their effect on attitude, subjective norm, and perceived behavioral control. In other words, the model dictates that variables external to the model (external variables) can affect behavior only through their effect on attitude, subjective norm, and perceived behavioral control levels.

According to many of the bureaucratic theories described in Chapter Three, support for reform in the acquisition work force should vary with certain personal characteristics. In the context of Army acquisition, these characteristics include:

- A worker's career group or professional affiliation (such as engineering, quality assurance, or the military).

- Rank (military) and grade level (civilian) (such as majors, lieutenant colonels, and colonels for military personnel, or GS-12, GS-15, and senior executive service (SES) for civilians).[6]

- Experience working in the acquisition system.

- Organizational affiliation with either the program management office or matrix organizations.[7] The matrix organizational structure used in Army acquisition is discussed below.

---

[5]Consider, for example, using the TPB to model voting behavior on a specific ballot initiative to place restrictions on nuclear power plants. In this case, the attitude having direct influence on the intention to vote is the attitude toward voting on the nuclear power ballot initiative. Other attitudes potentially of interest in affecting voting behavior might include attitude toward nuclear power, attitude toward voting, or attitude toward the construction of nuclear power plants (Bowman and Fishbein, 1978).

[6]In the civil service, GS refers to General Service and employees are classified at various GS levels (GS-11, GS-12, GS-13, etc.). The senior executive service (SES) refers to the classifications of senior-level civil service employees and managers. The SES is also made up of various levels (SES-1, SES-2, etc.).

[7]Other organizational variables might have included affiliation with a PEO-managed organization or a buying command, or specific PEO offices and buying commands. However, these variables were not found to be statistically significant.

In addition, specific training programs designed to facilitate reform may also have an effect. The TPB model argues that for an external variable to influence behavior it must have a significant effect on the level of attitude, subjective norm, and perceived behavioral control, which ultimately determine behavior.

For these six external variable categories, we examined sixteen variables. These variables are described in Table A.6.

While most of these six variable categories are easily understood, the organization and training categories require some additional description. The Army acquisition system employs the matrix form of management, which became popular in the 1970s and 1980s (Anderson, 1994; Bartlett and Ghoshal, 1990; Davis and Lawrence, 1978; Galbraith, 1971).

The matrix system separates key functions into separate management structures. These organizations are composed of two or more "divisions." Commonly there is a "product" division focused on building and marketing a product, complemented by a "functional" or "technical" division. In the Army context, the "product"-focused division is the Program Management Office (PM office). This office is made up of military and civilian personnel who oversee and manage the development and acquisition of a weapon system or other defense system. The functional side of the matrix is generally considered to support the product side of the matrix. These functions are more process oriented—they focus on providing a skill, technology, or service to the product side of the matrix in a certain prescribed or regulated manner. In the Army system these organizations are referred to as matrix organizations. They provide functional and technical assistance to the PM office in its management of acquisition programs and contracts. In the Army, matrix organizations provide assistance through the engineering, quality assurance, logistics, and contracting functions. This assistance can be technical in nature, such as testing and evaluation conducted by Army engineers, or more functional/process oriented, such as the evaluation of contracting provisions by personnel in the contracting function.

There are three major training programs that may have an effect on employee perspectives on reform: formal acquisition training, Integrated Product Team (IPT) training, and Road Show IV training.

Table A.6

External Variables Assessed by Category

Variable Category	Variable Name	Variable Code	Type of Variable	Variable Description
Career group	Engineering	ENG	Dummy	1 if engineering, 0 if not
	Quality assurance	QA	Dummy	1 if QA, 0 if not
	Logistics	LOG	Dummy	1 if logistics, 0 if not
	Contracting	CONT	Dummy	1 if contracting, 0 if not
	Military	MIL	Dummy	1 if military, 0 if not
Rank	Major and below	MAJ	Dummy	1 if major or below, 0 if not
	Lieutenant colonel	LTC	Dummy	1 if lieutenant colonel, 0 if not
	Colonel	COL	Dummy	1 if colonel, 0 if not
Grade level	Lower-grade	LG	Dummy	1 if GS-12 or below, 0 if not
	Mid-grade	MG	Dummy	1 if GS-13 or GS-14, 0 if not
	Upper-grade	UG	Dummy	1 if GS-15 or above, 0 if not
Experience	Under 20 years	UND20	Dummy	1 if under 20 years' experience, 0 if not
	Over 20 years	OVR20	Dummy	1 if over 20 years' experience, 0 if not
Organization	Program management	PM	Dummy	1 if in PM office, 0 if not
	Matrix organization	MATRIX	Dummy	1 if in matrix organization, 0 if not
Training	Acquisition training	AQTRAIN	Dummy	1 if had acquisition training, 0 if not
	IPT training	IPT	Dummy	1 if had IPT training, 0 if not
	Road Show IV training	RS4	Dummy	1 if had Road Show IV training, 0 if not

Formal acquisition training is conducted through the Defense Acquisition University and most commonly by the Defense Systems Management College (DSMC). These courses train employees on how to manage and operate within the defense acquisition system. The Army is currently encouraging the use of IPTs in the acquisition process and a series of training programs under way to encourage the various functions involved in the acquisition process to cooperate and "team." Finally, the Army has instituted a series of Road Show training programs to advance its reform agenda. One of these programs—Road Show IV—was directed at training employees how to discontinue using milspecs and standards and how to rewrite them into performance-based specifications. The effects of each of these training programs on reform behavior and its determinants were examined.

Do career group, rank, grade level, experience, organizational affiliation, and training matter in determining attitude, subjective norm, and perceived behavioral control? In other words, is there significant variation in these factors as a function of these external variables? Demonstrating the relationship between specific external variables and the five indicator variables ($A1$ and $A2$, S, and $P1$ and $P2$),[8] Table A.7 shows the results of regressions of the indicator variables on the complete set of external variables shown in Table A.6. Since the independent variables are dummy variables indicating membership in a given group, the change in the dependent variable associated with any given independent variable is relative to an excluded group. These excluded groups are:

- The effect of civilian career fields of engineering, quality assurance, logistics, or contracting is relative to military personnel (e.g., compared to the average value of attitude measure one for a member of the military, an engineer has an average attitude measure one score that is 0.74 lower).

---

[8]Ideally, the relationship between external variables and the single ATT, SN, and PBC factors should be examined. Due to limitations in the EQS software, factor scores for ATT and PBC could not be generated, so direct relationships between the external variables and the factors could not be estimated. As a consequence, the effect of external variables on each of the relevant indicator variables ($A1$, $A2$, $P1$, and $P2$) is calculated instead.

- The effect of being a lieutenant colonel or a colonel is relative to major or below.

- The effect of mid- or upper-grade civilian is relative to lower-grade civilian.

- The effect of having over 20 years' experience is relative to under 20 years' experience.

- The effect of affiliation with the PM office is relative to matrix organization affiliation.

- The effect of the three training variables is relative to not having participated in the training programs.

These results show that several career groups are associated with lower values for attitude measures one and two, subjective norm, and perceived behavioral control measures one and two.[9] Overall, the rank and grade-level groupings do not seem to be significantly associated with differences in the indicator variables.[10] Having over 20 years' experience is associated with a significant reduction in the level of both attitude measures. Affiliation with program management (PM) is associated with significantly higher scores for the attitude and subjective norm measures.

Participation in acquisition training programs, most commonly Defense Systems Management College (DSMC) or other Defense Acquisition University (DAU) courses, is significantly related only to a reduction in perceived behavioral control measure two. Taking IPT

---

[9]Specifically, engineers are related to lower values for all indicator variables (except P1) in comparison to military personnel. Quality assurance (QA) and logistics personnel, when compared to military personnel, are related to significantly lower values reported across all indicator variables. Contracting personnel are not significantly different from military personnel in their attitude, subjective norm, and perceived behavioral control levels.

[10]There are some significant relationships, but only colonels are associated with significantly lower perceived behavioral control measure two scores compared to majors and below, mid-grade civilians are associated with significantly lower perceived behavioral control measure two scores compared to lower-grade civilians, and upper-grade civilians are associated with lower subjective norm scores than lower-grade civilians.

Table A.7

Prediction of Reform *ATT*, *SN*, and *PBC* by External Variables: Regression Results

External Variable	A1	A2	S	P1	P2
			Dependent Variable		
Career group[a]					
Engineering	−0.74**	−0.73**	−0.66**	−0.26	−0.49**
Quality assurance	−1.59**	−1.79**	−1.22**	−0.73**	−1.37**
Logistics	−0.75**	−0.82**	−0.49**	−0.38*	−0.62**
Contracting	0.23	0.10	−0.10	0.12	0.18
Rank[b]					
Lt. colonel	−0.20	−0.12	−0.04	−0.13	−0.28
Colonel	−0.28	−0.22	−0.22	−0.12	−0.81**
Grade level[c]					
Mid-grade	−0.15	−0.08	0.14	−0.01	−0.22*
Upper-grade	−0.17	0.22	0.47**	0.04	−0.27
Experience[d]					
Over 20 years	−0.43**	−0.32**	−0.19	−0.23	−0.26*
Organization[e]					
Program management	0.28**	0.24**	0.28**	0.09	0.06
Training[f]					
Acquisition training	−0.03	−0.10	−0.06	−0.21	−0.22*
IPT training	0.25**	0.26**	0.18*	−0.06	0.05
Road Show IV	0.35**	0.19*	0.08	−0.15	−0.05
Constant	0.86**	1.21*	1.29**	0.32	0.58**
R-squared	0.11	0.13	0.07	0.03	0.07
F-statistic	15.11**	17.17**	9.15**	3.22**	8.50**
Sample size	1,653	1,653	1,653	1,653	1,653

*$p > .05$.
**$p > .01$.
[a]Relative to military personnel.
[b]Relative to majors and below.
[c]Relative to lower grades (GS-12) and below.
[d]Relative to less than 20 years' experience in acquisition.
[e]Relative to matrix (non-PM) personnel.
[f]Relative to not having specified training.

training[11] is associated with a significant increase in the attitude and subjective norm scores. In addition, having participated in Road Show IV is associated with significant increases in both measures of reform attitude.

Collapsing the external variables made up of more than one subgroup, Table A.8 shows the joint significance of the career group, rank, grade-level, and training variables in predicting the levels of the indicator variables (measures of attitude, subjective norm, and perceived behavioral control). The table reports F-tests of the joint significance of these variables in the prediction of the indicator variables. The career groups, jointly, are significantly related to all indicator variables ($p > .01$,[12] across attitude measures one and two; subjective norm; and perceived behavioral control measures one and two). The joint significance of the rank and grade-level variables, however, is lower. The rank variables are jointly significantly related to perceived behavioral control measure two only ($p > .05$). Grade level is jointly significantly related to subjective norm only ($p > .05$). The training variables are jointly significantly related to both attitude variables ($p > .01$).

Table A.8

F-Tests of Joint Significance of External Variable Groups

	A1	A2	S	P1	P2
Career group variables	24.88**	32.09**	13.91**	6.63**	18.05**
Military rank variables	0.67	0.41	0.39	0.20	4.19*
Civil grade-level variables	1.09	1.71	3.91*	0.03	2.56
Over 20 years	10.10**	6.98**	2.69	2.74	4.00*
Program management	7.96**	7.83**	11.33**	0.81	0.38
Training variables	7.25**	5.69**	2.58	2.38	1.74

*$p > .05$.
**$p > .01$.

---

[11]IPT training is discussed in more detail in Chapter Ten. The IPT training dummy variable is based on participation in training programs provided by any one of four sources: DSMC/DAU IPT training, externally provided (consultants, colleges, etc.), contractor-provided (prime contractors on a system), or internally provided (program office or buying command sponsored).

[12]The term $p > .01$ says that a test, such as the F-test or t-test, is significant at the 1 percent level. The term $p > .05$ says that a test is significant at the 5 percent level.

In addition, Table A.8 shows that experience level is significantly related to both attitude measures. Organizational affiliation is significantly related to attitude and subjective norm measures (p > .01, on the three indicator variables).

The primary objective of this section was to identify those external variables important in determining the level of reform attitude, subjective norm, and perceived behavioral control. Since the relationship between external variables and variation in these latent variables estimated in the LVM model could not be explicitly done, we have had to examine the relationship with each of the relevant indicator variables. How should one determine whether or not an external variable is important, especially if a variable is related to one indicator of a latent variable but not the other? This study uses a conservative approach to identify those external variables with an important effect on attitude, subjective norm, or perceived behavioral control. Only those external variables that are highly significant (p > .01) in the prediction of all indicators of a latent variable are identified as important. Using this rule of thumb, we conclude that career group is important in the prediction of each latent variable: attitude, subjective norm, and perceived behavioral control. Experience is important for attitude; organizational affiliation (PM versus non-PM) is important for attitude and subjective norm; and training is important for attitude.

Ajzen, I. (1991). "The Theory of Planned Behavior," *Organizational Behavior and Human Decision Processes*, Vol. 50, pp. 179–211.

———— and Fishbein, M. (1977). "Attitude-Behavior Relations: A Theoretical Analysis and Review of Empirical Research," *Psychological Bulletin*, Vol. 84, No. 5, pp. 888–918.

———— and ———— (1980). *Understanding Attitudes and Predicting Behavior*. Englewood Cliffs, NJ: Prentice Hall, Inc.

———— and Madden, T. (1986). "Prediction of Goal Directed Behavior: Attitudes, Intentions, and Perceived Behavioral Control," *Journal of Experimental Social Psychology*, Vol. 22, pp. 453–474.

Anderson, R. E. (1994). "Matrix Redux," *Business Horizons*, November–December 1994, pp. 6–10.

Army Materiel Command (1995). *Road Show IV Exercise Book: The Acquisition Challenge*. Alexandria, VA: Army Materiel Command.

Assistant Secretary of the Army (RDA) (1994). *Army Implementation Plan: Implementing the Report of the DoD Process Action Team on Military Specifications and Standards*. Report, Department of the Army, Department of Defense.

Bartlett, C. A., and Ghoshal, S. (1990). "Matrix Management: Not a Structure, a Frame of Mind," *Harvard Business Review*, July–August 1990, pp. 138–145.

Barzelay, M. (1992). *Breaking Through Bureaucracy.* Berkeley, CA: University of California Press.

Beer, M., Eisenstat, R. A., and Spector, B. (1990). "Why Change Programs Don't Produce Change," *Harvard Business Review,* November–December 1990, pp. 158–166.

Bender, B. (1995). "Army Acquisition Officials Give Integrated Product Teams Good Marks," *Inside the Army,* September 18, 1995, pp. 7, 12.

Bentler, P. M. (1995). *EQS Structural Equations Program Manual.* Encino, CA: Multivariate Software, Inc.

———, and Wu, E. J. C. (1995). *EQS for Macintosh User's Guide.* Encino, CA: Multivariate Software, Inc.

Bingaman, J., Gansler, J., and Kupperman, R. (1991). *Integrating Commercial and Military Technologies for National Strength: An Agenda for Change.* Report, CSIS Steering Committee on Security and Technology.

Blais, A., and Dion, S. (eds.) (1991). *The Budget-Maximizing Bureaucrat: Appraisals and Evidence.* Pittsburgh: University of Pittsburgh Press.

Bowman, C. H., and Fishbein, M. (1978). "Understanding Public Reaction to Energy Proposals: An Application of the Fishbein Model," *Journal of Applied Social Psychology,* Vol. 8, No. 4, pp. 319–340.

Buchanan, B. (1974). "Government Managers, Business Executives, and Organizational Commitment," *Public Administration Review,* July/August 1974, pp. 339–347.

Byrne, B. M. (1994). *Structural Equation Modeling with EQS and EQS/Windows.* Thousand Oaks, CA: Sage.

Caiden, G. E. (1994). "Administrative Reform," in R. Baker (ed.), *Comparative Public Management.* Westport, CT: Praeger Publishers.

Campbell, S. J. C., and Naulls, D. (1991). "The Limits of the Budget-Maximizing Theory: Some Evidence from Officials' Views of Their

Roles and Careers," in A. Blais and S. Dion (eds.), *The Budget-Maximizing Bureaucrat: Appraisals and Evidence.* Pittsburgh: University of Pittsburgh Press.

Carnegie Commission on Science, Technology, and Government (1993). *New Thinking and American Defense Technology.* New York: Carnegie Commission on Science, Technology, and Government.

Coopers and Lybrand, and TASC. (1994). *The DoD Regulatory Cost Premium: A Quantitative Assessment.* Report prepared for Secretary of Defense William J. Perry.

Davis, S. M., and Lawrence, P. R. (1978). "Problems of Matrix Organizations," *Harvard Business Review,* May–June 1978, pp. 131–142.

Decker, G. F. (1994). "Modernization Is the Key to 21st Century Readiness," *Army,* pp. 39–44.

Department of the Army (1994). *Acquisition Oversight and Review Process Action Team First Draft Report.* Report, Department of the Army, Department of Defense.

Department of Defense (1989). *Report of the Defense Science Board on Use of Commercial Components in Military Equipment.* DSB Report, Department of Defense.

Department of Defense, Process Action Team on Military Specifications and Standards (1994). *Blueprint for Change: Toward a National Production Base.* Process Action Team Report, Department of Defense.

Dertouzos, J. N., Schmidt, C., Benjamin, B., and Finegold, D. (1998). *Facilitating Effective Reform in Army Acquisition.* Santa Monica, CA: RAND, DB-233-A.

DeVellis, B. M., Blalock, S. J., and Sandler, R. S. (1990). "Predicting Participation in Cancer Screening: The Role of Perceived Behavioral Control," *Journal of Applied Social Psychology,* Vol. 20, No. 8, pp. 639–660.

DiIulio, J. J., Garvey, G., and Kettl, D. F. (1993). *Improving Government Performance: An Owner's Manual.* Washington, D.C.: Brookings Institution.

Downs, A. (1967). *Inside Bureaucracy.* Boston: Little, Brown and Company.

Dreilinger, C. (1994). "Why Management Fads Fizzle," *Business Horizons,* November–December 1994, pp. 11–15.

Drucker, P. F. (1973). "Managing the Public Service Institution," *Public Interest,* Vol. 33 (Fall), pp. 43–60.

———— (1995). "Really Reinventing Government," *The Atlantic Monthly,* February 1995, pp. 49–61.

Duck, J. D. (1993). "Managing Change: The Art of Balancing," *Harvard Business Review,* November–December 1993, pp. 109–118.

Eagly, A. H., and Chaiken, S. (1993). *The Psychology of Attitudes.* Fort Worth, TX: Harcourt Brace Jovanovich College Publishers.

Fishbein, M. (1979). "A Theory of Reasoned Action: Some Applications and Implications," in H. Howe and M. Page (eds.), *Nebraska Symposium on Motivation.* Lincoln, NE: University of Nebraska Press.

————, Chan, D. K. S., O'Reilly, K., Schnell, D., Wood, R., Beeker, C., and Cohn, D. (1992). "Attitudinal and Normative Factors as Determinants of Gay Men's Intentions to Perform AIDS-Related Sexual Behaviors: A Multisite Analysis," *Journal of Applied Social Psychology,* Vol. 22, No. 13, pp. 999–1011.

Galbraith, J. R. (1971). "Matrix Organization Designs: How to Combine Functional and Project Forms," *Business Horizons,* February 1971, pp. 29–40.

Garvin, D. A. (1993). "Building a Learning Organization," *Harvard Business Review,* July–August 1993, pp. 78–91.

Gleckman, H., Garland, S., Melcher, R., and Weber, J. (1995). "Downsizing Government," *Business Week,* January 23, 1995, pp. 34–41.

Gore, A. (1993). *From Red Tape to Results: Creating a Government That Works Better and Costs Less.* Report, National Performance Review.

Goss, T., Pascale, R., and Athos, A. (1993). "The Reinvention Roller Coaster: Risking the Present for a Powerful Future," *Harvard Business Review,* November–December 1993, pp. 97–108.

Hall, G., Rosenthal, J., and Wade, J. (1993). "How to Make Reengineering Really Work," *Harvard Business Review,* November–December 1993, pp. 119–131.

Hammer, M., and Champy, J. (1993). *Reengineering the Corporation: A Manifesto for Business Revolution.* New York: Harper Business/HarperCollins Publishers, Inc.

Kelman, S. (1990). *Procurement and Public Management.* Washington, D.C.: The AEI Press.

Knott, J. H., and Miller, G. J. (1987). *Reforming Bureaucracy: The Politics of Institutional Choice.* Englewood Cliffs, NJ: Prentice-Hall, Inc.

Kotter, J. P. (1995). "Leading Change: Why Transformation Efforts Fail," *Harvard Business Review,* March–April 1995, pp. 59–67.

Light, P. (1994). "Surviving Reinvention," *Government Executive,* June 1994, p. 55.

Lipsky, M. (1980). *Street-Level Bureaucracy.* New York: Russel-Sage.

March, J. G., and Olsen, J. P. (1989). *Rediscovering Institutions: The Organizational Basis of Politics.* New York: The Free Press.

Melamid, E., and Luck, J. (1995). "On Fixing the Bureaucracy: Getting the Questions Right." Unpublished draft, RAND Graduate School.

Migue, J. L., and Belanger, G. (1974). "Toward a General Theory of Managerial Discretion," *Public Choice,* Vol. 17, pp. 29–47.

Netemeyer, R. G., and Burton, S. (1990). "Examining the Relationships Between Voting Behavior, Intention, Perceived Behavioral

Control, and Expectation," *Journal of Applied Social Psychology*, Vol. 20, pp. 661–680.

Niskanen, W. A. (1971). *Bureaucracy and Representative Government*. Chicago: Aldine Atherton.

———— (1991). "A Reflection on Bureaucracy and Representative Government," in A. Blais and S. Dion (eds.), *The Budget-Maximizing Bureaucrat: Appraisals and Evidence*. Pittsburgh: University of Pittsburgh Press.

Osborne, D., and Gaebler, T. (1992). *Reinventing Government: How the Entrepreneurial Spirit Is Transforming the Public Sector*. New York: Addison-Wesley Publishing Company, Inc.

Ouchi, W. G. (1980). "Markets, Bureaucracies and Clans," *Administrative Science Quarterly*, Vol. 25 (March), pp. 129–141.

Pedhazur, E. J. (1982). "Introduction to Linear Structural Relations (LISREL)," in E. J. Pedhazur (ed.), *Multiple Regression in Behavioral Research*. Fort Worth, TX: Harcourt Brace College Publishers.

Perry, J. L., and Porter, L. W. (1982). "Factors Affecting the Context for Motivation in Public Organizations," *Academy of Management Review*, Vol. 7, No. 1, pp. 89–98.

Perry, W. J. (1994a). *Acquisition Reform: A Mandate for Change*. Washington, D.C.: Department of Defense.

———— (1994b). *Specifications and Standards—A New Way of Doing Business*. Washington, D.C.: Department of Defense.

Peters, B. G., and Savoie, D. J. (1994). "Civil Service Reform: Misdiagnosing the Patient," *Public Administration Review*, Vol. 45, No. 5, pp. 418–425.

Petty, R. E., and Cacioppo, J. T. (1981). *Attitudes and Persuasion: Classic and Contemporary Approaches*. Dubuque, IA: Wm. C. Brown Company.

Posner, B. G., and Rothstein, L. R. (1994). "Reinventing the Business of Government: An Interview with Change Catalyst David Osborne," *Harvard Business Review*, May–June 1994, pp. 133–143.

Reinecke, J., Schmidt, P., and Ajzen, I. (1996). "Application of the Theory of Planned Behavior to Adolescents Condom Use: A Panel Study," *Journal of Applied Social Psychology*, Vol. 26, No. 9, pp. 749–772.

Reynolds, L. (1994). Can Government Be Reinvented?" *Management Review*, pp. 14–21.

Sabatier, P. A., Loomis, J., and McCarthy, C. (1995). "Hierarchical Controls, Professional Norms, Local Constituencies, and Budget Maximization: An Analysis of U.S. Forest Service Planning Decisions," *American Journal of Political Science*, Vol. 39, No. 1, pp. 204–242.

Salomon, L. E. (1994). "At AMC the Future Begins Today," *Army*, October 1994, pp. 69–75.

Schifter, D. E., and Ajzen, I. (1985). "Intention, Perceived Control, and Weight Loss: An Application of the Theory of Planned Behavior," *Journal of Personality and Social Psychology*, Vol. 49, No. 3, pp. 843–851.

Sheppard, B. H., Hartwick, J., and Warshaw, P. R. (1988). "The Theory of Reasoned Action: A Meta-Analysis of Past Research with Recommendations for Modifications and Future Research," *Journal of Consumer Research*, Vol. 15 (December), pp. 325–343.

Shoop, T. (1995). "Reinventing Reinvention," *Government Executive*, January 1995, pp. 17–20.

Simons, R. (1995). "Control in the Age of Empowerment," *Harvard Business Review*, March–April 1995, pp. 80–88.

Tichy, N. M., and Sherman, S. (1993). *Control Your Destiny or Someone Else Will: Lessons in Mastering Change—the Principles Jack Welch Is Using to Revolutionize General Electric*. New York: HarperCollins/Harper Business Publishers.

Tullock, G. (1965). *The Politics of Bureaucracy*. Washington, D.C.: Public Affairs Press.

Weber, M. (1962). "Bureaucracy," in *Max Weber: Essays in Sociology*. New York: Oxford University Press.

Williamson, O. E. (1989). "Transaction Cost Economics," in R. Schmalensee and R. D. Willig (eds.), *Handbook of Industrial Organization*. New York: Elsevier Science Publishers.

—————— (ed.) (1990). *Organization Theory: From Chester Barnard to the Present and Beyond.* New York: Oxford University Press.

Wilson, J. Q. (1989). *Bureaucracy.* New York: Basic Books.

Womack, J. P., and Jones, D. T. (1994). "From Lean Production to the Lean Enterprise," *Harvard Business Review,* March–April 1994, pp. 93–103.

——————, ——————, and Roos, D. (1990). *The Machine That Changed the World: The Story of Lean Production.* New York: Rawson Associates/Harper Perennial.